THE TIMES

train
your brain
Puzzle Book

First published in 2008 by Collins

An imprint of HarperCollinsPublishers
77-85 Fulham Palace Road
Hammersmith, London
W6 8JB

www.collins.co.uk

Copyright © Puzzler Media Ltd 2008, www.puzzler.com

Reprint 10 9 8 7 6 5 4 3 2 1

The Times is a registered trademark of Times Newspapers Ltd

ISBN 978-0-00-728159-6

A catalogue record for this book is available from the British Library

Printed and bound in Great Britain by Clays Ltd, St Ives plc.

Mixed Sources
Product group from well-managed
forests and other controlled sources
www.fsc.org Cert no. SW-COC-1806
© 1996 Forest Stewardship Council

FSC is a non-profit international organisation established to promote the
responsible management of the world's forests. Products carrying the FSC
label are independently certified to assure consumers that they come
from forests that are managed to meet the social, economic and
ecological needs of present and future generations.

Find out more about HarperCollins and the environment at
www.harpercollins.co.uk/green

Contents

INTRODUCTION

Puzzles are good for your mental health. Research has shown that daily exercises can boost memory and concentration skills. Studies have found a correlation between increased levels of mental stimulation and reduced risk of dementia, while simple acts such as reading aloud, doing arithmetic or solving a puzzle can increase blood flow to the prefrontal cortex, which stimulates activity in the rest of the brain.

Analysis also shows that connections between brain cells can be reinforced by repetition, suggesting that the brain is like a muscle that needs regular stretching.

Here is a collection of daily brain-training exercises to improve the resilience of your mind. Variety, not difficulty, is key so they should prove more fun than maths homework. Enjoy.

Michael Harvey, Features Editor, *The Times*

Workout
1-190

WORKOUT 1

Wordsearch

TIME

How quickly can you find the five themed words in each grid?

CAKES

R	I	G	J	L	C	F
R	I	A	L	C	E	V
X	Z	T	S	E	Y	E
N	T	E	P	M	N	Q
D	A	A	B	O	U	H
U	G	U	C	W	B	O
W	K	S	T	A	R	T

FRUIT

E	L	P	P	A	P	F
P	N	A	B	Y	I	T
F	A	W	A	G	E	L
Z	S	P	N	J	X	B
R	G	R	A	P	E	M
C	U	Q	N	Y	I	K
H	V	O	A	G	A	D

Splits

TIME

Can you rearrange each of these sets of letter blocks into a word?

1 RY SCO DI VE
2 RAT TO ED LE
3 OR LIC IT SO

4 TU LO DE NGI
5 ER WH HEV IC

Cell Blocks

TIME

Fill the grid by drawing blocks along the gridlines. Each block must be square or rectangular and must contain the number of squares indicated by the digit inside it. Each block must contain only one digit.

8

Sudoku

TIME

Place a number in each empty square so that each row, each column and each 2x2 block contains all the numbers from 1-4.

Add Up

TIME

If the number in each circle is the sum of the two below it, how quickly can you figure out the top number? Try this one in your head, before writing anything down.

WORKOUT 3

TIME

Codeword

Can you crack the code and fill in the crossword grid? Each letter of the alphabet makes at least one appearance in the grid, and is represented by the same number wherever it appears. The four letters we've decoded should help you to identify other letters and words in the grid.

A B C D E F G H I J K L M N O P Q R S T U V W X Y Z

| 1 | 2 | 3 | 4 | 5 | 6 | 7 | 8 E | 9 | 10 | 11 S | 12 N | 13 |
| 14 | 15 | 16 | 17 W | 18 | 19 | 20 | 21 | 22 | 23 | 24 | 25 | 26 |

Spot the Sum

TIME

In each of these boxes, one of the numbers is the sum of two others. Can you spot the sum?

1

27 33 20 9 19
14 16 15 12

2

10 1 27 7 33
12 21 18 4

3

38 18 5 11 3
25 12 31 21

4

5 6 28 9 24
13 20 31 34

10

Memory Jog

Spend two minutes memorising this list of twenty words, then see how many of them you can recall on a separate piece of paper in another two minutes.

COURAGE	BLUE	BLITHELY	ANTIQUES
DRILL	SHARPEN	WAGON	MESH
HATSTAND	SITCOM	TEAPOT	PURPOSE
MANNERS	PLASTER	PANTOMIME	SPILL
PARTICULAR	CONTINUE	CELLAR	FORTUNE

Pyramid

Each answer except the first uses all the letters – usually in a different order – from the previous answer plus one extra letter.

TIME

1 Personal pronoun

2 That thing

3 Neckwear

4 Row of seats

5 Sluggish

6 Eye's light-sensitive
   membrane

7 Piece of ground for
   military use

8 Hold someone
   back from action

9 Apprehending

WORKOUT 5

Futoshiki

Fill the blank squares so that each row and column contains all the numbers 1, 2, 3 and 4. Use the given numbers and the symbols that tell you if the number in the square is larger (>) or smaller (<) than the number next to it.

Initials

If ITHOTN (Oscar-winning film) is *IN THE HEAT OF THE NIGHT*, what do these initials represent?

1 WICW (George Formby song)

2 TBM (Nursery rhyme)

3 SAKP (Traditional British dish)

4 TLTWATW (Children's novel)

5 RLYL (Famous tongue twister)

Town to Town

Can you travel from **Croydon** to **Orlando** by removing or adding one letter at each stage from the definitions below, which are consequent anagrams?

1 American vulture

2 Musical piece with a recurring theme

3 Room "barrier"

4 Item of fishing equipment

5 Thoroughfare

6 Embellish

7 ___ Rat, Channel 4 star

Fitword

When all of the listed words have been placed correctly in the grid, which one is left over?

3 letters
Cud
Ego
Emu
Gym
Hit
Jaw
Owe
Sow
Wax
Web

4 letters
Bomb
Defy
Limp
Luck
Nest
Pair
Sawn
Zany

5 letters
Annoy
Aorta
Aroma
Media
Merit
Minus

6 letters
Obtain
Rotund

Six Pack

Can you place digits in the empty triangles, so that the numbers in each hexagon add up to 25? Only single digits between 1 and 9 can be used, and no two numbers in any hexagon may be the same.

WORKOUT 7

Pathfinder

TIME

Beginning with JUDGES, and moving up, down, left or right, one letter at a time, can you trace a path of seventeen Old Testament books?

E	D	L	E	C	I	T	I	V	H	A
U	E	K	I	U	O	N	A	E	L	I
T	Z	E	B	S	J	J	H	R	E	M
E	R	J	O	A	H	O	S	E	J	H
N	O	L	A	B	A	U	H	M	I	A
O	I	E	K	K	J	G	E	S	C	I
M	N	E	K	U	U	D	M	E	A	D
Y	A	X	O	A	H	L	A	N	H	A
N	D	H	D	I	N	A	H	T	O	B
A	H	A	U	S	Z	E	P	A	T	I
M	U	I	M	E	H	E	N	S	N	O

Number Jig

TIME

Which one of the listed numbers won't fit in each of these mini grids?

256
324
346
454
514

469
496
619
691
914

2132
2223
2310
3131
3210

Copycats

TIME

Choose the answer that best copies the pattern.

READ is to WRITE as LISTEN is to: Ear • Mime • Look • Speak • Hear

DOG is to KENNEL as SQUIRREL is to: Nest • Holt • Tree • Drey • Hole

JAM is to JAR as TEA is to: Cup • Pot • Caddy • Can • Urn

MILE is to MOLE as MOLE is to: Male • More • Mule • Sole • Mire

Dominoes

Solve the clues then write the six-letter answers into the dominoes. You must work out whether each word fits in clockwise or anticlockwise, so that the connecting letters of the dominoes all match up.

1 Princess ___, the late Duchess of Kent

2 ___ Eccleston, Formula 1 boss

3 ___ Steptoe, Harold's father

4 Mother ___, Calcutta nun

5 *King* ___, Elvis song and movie

6 ___ Schwarzenegger, film star and Governor of California

Sudoku

Use your powers of reasoning to place numbers in the grid, so that each row, each column and each 3x3 block contains the numbers 1-9.

	9	4	3		7	8	2	
2				5				3
3	8						7	4
		7	8		4	5		
	4		2		9		1	
		3				1		
			6	4	5			
	5	2				9	4	

Codewords

If **HERD is 1234** and **ARMY is 5367**, how quickly can you work out these collective nouns? You should identify more letters as you go along.

1 8 1 5 3 6

2 8 3 5 9 1

3 9 10 5 3 6

4 6 11 3 4 2 3

5 12 3 13 4 2

WORKOUT 9

Mini Fit

Which one of the listed words won't fit in each of these mini grids?

ACT
APT
CAP
TIP
TIC

DOE
DOR
ORE
RED
ROD

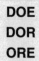

FIVE
FLAT
LAIR
TILE
VIAL

CROW
DOVE
ERNE
ROOK
WREN

Wordsearch

Hidden in this wordsearch grid are eighteen musical instruments.

A	P	T	L	B	A	N	J	O
R	S	E	G	N	O	G	P	N
I	I	N	A	P	M	I	T	A
S	T	I	T	P	C	U	T	I
M	L	R	R	C	B	E	V	P
D	F	A	O	A	P	J	I	E
R	H	L	B	M	L	H	O	O
U	O	C	U	M	B	O	L	B
M	F	R	Y	T	Y	O	I	O
S	T	O	L	L	E	C	N	V
G	U	I	T	A	R	B	G	E

Scramble

What EU capital cities can be made from each of these sets of scrambled letters?

1 MORE

2 PAIRS

3 HASTEN

4 NO GAP HENCE

5 CHERUB SAT

6 PUB DATES

7 MADE SMART

8 STAB A RIVAL

16

Small Change

Can you change one letter of each of these words to make five new words with a common theme?

1 LORD • LOVER • FLAT • SENT • NEXUS

2 HOSE • DAIRY • LILT • IRKS • PALSY

3 FOLD • SALVER • TIC • ICON • LEAF

4 CABLE • CHAIN • DUSK • CREST • PRESSER

Opposites Attract

Can you sort each set of letter blocks into two words with opposite meanings?

1 LL TY FU EMP

2 ART FI SH NI ST

3 LE DIF SI CU FI MP LT

4 GUE ISE PR VA EC

Kakuro

Simple addition and a bit of logical thinking will solve this one. You must write a digit in each white square so that the digits in each across section add up to the total in the triangle to the left, and the digits in each column add up to the total in the triangle above. 1-9 are the only digits to use and, although you may find a digit repeated in a row, it must not be repeated in the same section. We've solved one section for you.

WORKOUT 11

Arroword

Just follow the arrows to write your answers in the grid. A handful of anagram clues will get you thinking differently.

	▼		▼		▼			▼	
CHEEPS (anag)		Thick mist		Sullivan's operetta partner		Small ocean		Makes less strong	Variety of polecat
IMPOSER (anag) ▶						▼		Grass road-edging	▼
Spider's flytrap		Edge of a hat		Go away, depart				▼	
▶			▼	Decorate (a cake)	BREAK (anag)				
Offence, unlawful act ▶			▼			Make mistakes ▶			
				ANGER (anag)					
▶ Elegant, stylish	Thaw ▶				Part of a tennis match				

Vowel Play

Can you replace the missing vowels to complete the names of these vegetables?

1 C R R T
2 P T T
3 L T T C
4 P
5 L K
6 K L
7 N N
8 C L R Y
9 R D S H
10 B T R T

Smart Sums

Try to avoid writing down anything but the final answers to these calculations...

1 Sides on a pentagon x different letters in CABBAGES

2 Squares on a chessboard ÷ quarts in a gallon

3 States in the USA – baker's dozen

4 Consonants in YELLOW + events in a heptathlon

Egg-Timer 〔TIME 〕

To answer these clues you have to remove a letter from the previous answer and (if necessary) rearrange the letters to get the new answer. When you pass clue 5, you have to do the opposite – adding a letter each time. We have put in one answer to help you.

3 **R A S H**

1 Red suit of cards
2 Divide up among friends
3 ~~Allergy spots~~
4 Powdery fire remains
5 ___ good ___ gold, saying
6 Area of salt water
7 Round green vegetables
8 Digging tool
9 Black suit of cards

Mobile Code 〔TIME 〕

If FEZ is 339 on this phone keypad, which items of headgear have the following numbers?

1	2 ABC	3 DEF
4 GHI	5 JKL	6 MNO
7 PQRS	8 TUV	9 WXYZ
*	0	#

1 227
2 23738
3 726262
4 874529
5 269537

Four by Four 〔TIME 〕

How quickly can you solve this mini crossword?

	1	2	3	4
5				
6				
7				

ACROSS

1 Sliding door-lock
5 Long operatic solo
6 Converse
7 Berry used to flavour gin

DOWN

1 Nocturnal flyers
2 Of the mouth
3 Air bed
4 Extract

19

WORKOUT 13

Set Square

Place one each of the digits 1-9 in the grid to make the sums work. We've put in some of the numbers to start you off. Sums should be solved from left to right, or from top to bottom.

In and Out

Without changing the order of the letters, add or remove one letter each time to leave a (different) new complete word and put the added or removed letters in their respective boxes to find **an accurate small version of a car** reading down the boxes.

CARESS

ACHE

HEARD

RIFE

SCRAM

RAMP

CORNER

BRAN

CEASE

BLIND

Box Wise

Can you place the three-letter groups in the boxes, so that neighbouring boxes always make a six-letter word, like PAR-DON or DON-ATE? We've placed one group to start you off.

COR	NCE	REP	~~TEE~~	TRA
LAY	ORY	SET	THE	VEL
MAN	OUT			

Mini Jigsaw

Fit the pieces in the grid to spell out a type of bird in each row.

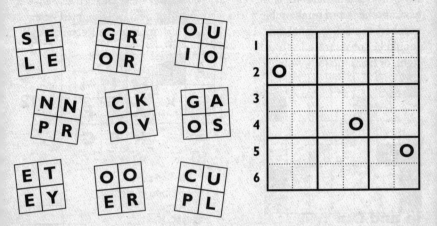

Killer Sudoku

The normal rules of Sudoku apply. Place a digit from 1-9 in each empty square so that each row, column and 3x3 block contains all the digits from 1-9. In addition, the digits in each inner shape (marked by dots) must add up to the number in the top corner of that box. No digit can be repeated within an inner shape.

Staircase

When these agriculture words are correctly fitted in the rows of the grid, another word on the subject will appear down the diagonal staircase.

ARABLE   **FARMER**   **YIELD**

CROPS   **HAYRICK**

DROVERS   **PIGLET**

Number Sequence

What number should come next in these sequences?

1 1, 7, 7, 13, 19, 31, ?

2 3, 3, 5, 4, 4, 3, 5, ?

3 4, 12, 44, 172, 684, ?

4 1, 1, 2, 6, 24, 120, 720, ?

5 1, 4, 13, 40, 121, 364, ?

Word Builder

Using the nine letters provided, can you answer these clues? Every answer must include the highlighted letter T. Which museum in Russia uses all nine letters?

H	I	M
A	T	E
R	E	G

5 Letters
Striped wildcat
Angry
Power
Consumer
Boat Race crew

6 Letters
Amass
Any of two
Profession
Warming appliance
Spat

7 Letters
Type of jazz
More muscular
Arab leader's domain

8 Letters
Move abroad
National history

Wild Words

What well-known phrases and expressions are suggested by these word pictures?

❶ THINK THINK

❷ ROTHECLOCKCK

❸

❹ BEAN

Fare's Fair

TIME

Find two words of the same sound but different spelling to satisfy each two-element clue, then decide which of the pair goes where in the grid to discover **a story in episodes**, reading down the arrowed column.

Civic leader's horse

Reported the bells rang

Painful tool

Flower in lines

Hold back money-order

Correct way to put pen to paper

Elimination

TIME

All but two of the listed words fall into one of the four categories. Put these leftover words together, and what phrase do they make?

CATEGORIES Dairy • Words following HAND (eg Held) • Gases • Boxing terms

Spar	Whey	Shake	Well	Yogurt	Ropes
Cuff	Neon	Some	Oxygen	Gloves	Brie
Done	Cheese	Argon	Corner	Made	
Set	Ring	Milk	Methane	Hydrogen	

WORKOUT 17

Niners

Form four nine-letter words using all twelve listed "syllables" (without altering the order of the letters in each "syllable"). Then enter them in the grid in the right order to reveal **a small branch** reading down the **left-hand** column.

ANT	DOL	ESC
GON	IDE	IER
INE	LDW	LEG
OPE	TEL	WOR

Memory Jog

Spend two minutes memorising this list of twenty words, then see how many of them you can recall on a separate piece of paper.

MEANDER	CHORTLE	CLING	SLAT	EXTRA
CUMMER-BUND	WHIM	BILL	BUBBLE	BENCH
	EERILY	BESIDE	ARROW	
STAMP	CLOWN	FESTIVAL	JUSTLY	
CERTAINLY	MAGPIE	MELTING		

Cell Blocks

Fill the grid by drawing blocks along the gridlines. Each block must be square or rectangular and must contain the number of squares indicated by the digit inside it. Each block must contain only one digit.

24

Sudoku

TIME

Place a number in each empty square so that each row, each column and each 2x2 block contains all the numbers from 1-4.

	2	3	
3			2
1			3
	3	1	

2			4
	4	2	
	1	4	
4			1

	2	3	
3			2
2			4
	4	2	

Add Up

TIME

If the number in each circle is the sum of the two below it, how quickly can you figure out the top number? Try this one in your head, before writing anything down.

25

TIME

Codeword

Can you crack the code and fill in the crossword grid? Each letter of the alphabet makes at least one appearance in the grid, and is represented by the same number wherever it appears. The four letters we've decoded should help you to identify other letters and words in the grid.

Copycats

Choose the answer that best copies the pattern.

TIME

TEAPOT is to POUR as KEY is to: Skeleton • Ring • Door • Open • Fob

UMBRELLA is to RAIN as PARASOL is to: Beach • Water • Sun • Cloud • Shade

DABC is to ABCD as SPQR is to: QPRS • SRPQ • RPQS • PQRS • QRSP

PILOT is to FLY as CHAUFFEUR is to: Sail • Drive • Steer • Car • Limousine

POET is to TOPE as PAST is to: Taps • Mind • Spat • Pats • Asps

Splits

Can you rearrange each of these sets of letter blocks into a word?

1 TE EFS BE AK
2 LI ED MIT UN
3 ANT RE ND DU

4 GN URE AT SI
5 ER GO OTH DM

Shape Up

Can you arrange these five-letter shapes into their correct
positions in the grid so that ten **artists** read down the columns?

WORKOUT 21

Futoshiki TIME

Fill the blank squares so that each row and column contains all the numbers 1, 2, 3 and 4. Use the given numbers and the symbols that tell you if the number in the square is larger (>) or smaller (<) than the number next to it.

Scramble TIME

What items of footwear can be made from each of these sets of scrambled letters?

1 HOSE

2 TAPS

3 TAKES

4 TRIAGE

5 BUG ROE

6 RIPPLES

7 ALLIED REPS

8 LINNET GLOW

Pet Talk TIME

Which numbered photo has been taken?

28

Fitword

TIME

When all of the listed words have been placed correctly in the grid, which one is left over?

4 letters
Alms
Drat
Holt
Imam
Mall
Ugly

5 letters
Agile
Kitty
Scout
Shade
Stoke

6 letters
Costly
Creamy

7 letters
Acronym
~~Immoral~~

9 letters
Cascading
Disembark

Mind the Gap

TIME

Can you place a well-known three-letter word in the spaces of each row to complete the seven-letter word? Do it correctly, and the shaded letters should spell out an African creature.

T	E				U	S
A				E	M	Y
A	C				A	T
A				A	N	T
F	O	R				R
I	N	S				D
A	F				M	S
A	W	A				G

WORKOUT 23

Pathfinder

TIME

Beginning with PIRATE SHIP, and moving up, down, left or right, one letter at a time, can you trace a path of seventeen types of boat?

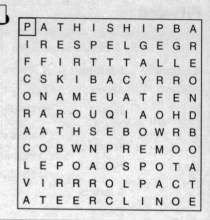

P	A	T	H	I	S	H	I	P	B	A
I	R	E	S	P	E	L	G	E	G	R
F	F	I	R	T	T	A	L	L	E
C	S	K	I	B	A	C	Y	R	R	O
O	N	A	M	E	U	A	T	F	E	N
R	A	R	O	U	Q	I	A	O	H	D
A	A	T	H	S	E	B	O	W	R	B
C	O	B	W	N	P	R	E	M	O	O
L	E	P	O	A	O	S	P	O	T	A
V	I	R	R	R	O	L	P	A	C	T
A	T	E	E	R	C	L	I	N	O	E

Soundalikes

TIME

Can you complete each of these sentences with two words that sound alike, but are spelt differently?

1 Little Jimmy ___ the ball ___ the hoop.

2 ___ Fido cut his ___ on some glass in the park.

3 '___ can I ___ my new shoes?' she cried.

Honeycomb

TIME

Write the six-letter answers clockwise round their respective cell-numbers, starting at the arrowed cell. On completion, you will find that the unclued answers (10 and 11) will reveal **the author of** *Nineteen Eighty-four*.

1 University award
2 Servant performing menial tasks
3 Look out!
4 *The Origin of Species* author
5 He shrinks from danger
6 Folk
7 Preaching "box" in a church
8 Picnic basket
9 Sawn timber

30

Set Square

TIME

Place one each of the digits 1-9 in the grid to make the sums work. We've put in some of the numbers to start you off. Sums should be solved from left to right, or from top to bottom.

Sudoku

TIME

Use your powers of reasoning to place numbers in the grid, so that each row, each column and each 3x3 block contains the numbers 1-9.

					4	5		
6			7	8			1	
5			6					4
	5	9		7				
	8	7		3		2	5	
				9		4	7	
7					9			6
	3			6	7			8
		8	3					

Initials

TIME

If **ITHOTN** (Oscar-winning film) is *IN THE HEAT OF THE NIGHT*, what do these initials represent?

1 AFINIAFI (Proverb)

2 TOCS (Dickens novel)

3 HFB (Fawlty Towers catchphrase)

4 OFOTCN (Jack Nicholson film)

5 BABP (Dessert)

Fix Six TIME

The six **authors** listed will fit into this pattern of six adjoining hexagons. All are entered clockwise from a triangle to be discovered. Adjoining triangles always contain the same letter. The **P** and **T** give you a start.

BRONTË	O'BRIEN
DEXTER	RANKIN
JEROME	UPDIKE

Wordsearch TIME

Hidden in this wordsearch grid are fifteen Winnie the Pooh words.

D	K	W	L	W	O	H	P	C
O	A	I	I	R	U	J	C	H
O	N	H	O	N	E	Y	X	R
W	G	O	D	V	N	E	F	I
O	A	R	E	G	G	I	T	S
E	E	Y	O	R	E	I	E	T
D	C	N	Q	A	B	T	E	O
R	N	U	I	B	C	L	A	P
G	U	W	A	B	G	R	L	H
Y	O	R	K	I	O	S	E	E
H	B	B	P	Z	M	R	D	R

Picture Pair TIME

Which two pictures are identical?

Number Jig

Which one of the listed numbers won't fit in each of these mini grids?

234
372
439
749
792

158
165
567
815
826

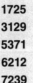

1725
3129
5371
6212
7239

Small Change

Can you change one letter of each of these words to make five new words with a common theme?

1 SCORE • PART • FUN • CARE • PIT

2 TURN • LACE • FOOL • FOND • MORE

3 STORE • ROUND • DON • GRIM • DUNCE

4 SHORES • SKINT • KILO • MOWN • PRESS

Kakuro

Simple addition and a bit of logical thinking will solve this one. You must write a digit in each white square so that the digits in each across section add up to the total in the triangle to the left, and the digits in each column add up to the total in the triangle above. 1-9 are the only digits to use and, although you may find a digit repeated in a row, it must not be repeated in the same section. We've solved one section for you.

WORKOUT 27

Arroword

Just follow the arrows to write your answers in the grid. A handful of anagram clues will get you thinking differently.

Convince or guarantee ▼	Pig's enclosure ▼		Projecting rock ▼	ELM (anag)	▼	Hand-held percussion instruments	Sumptuous meal
Easy-to-peel citrus fruit ▶				▼		LIMES (anag)	▼
Stick (out)	Gossip		RESET (anag) ▶			▼	
▶		▼	Colour (hair)	Vice ▶			
Aircraft location system		▼		US spy organisation (inits) ▶			
▶			Ellipses ▶				
▶	Depend (on)	Large brown seaweed		Full collection ▶			

Take Five

The three answers in this mini-crossword read the same across and down. We've clued the three answers, but not in the right order. See how quickly you can solve it.

Permit

The shinbone

Commonplace, trite

Two of a Kind

Can you sort each set of letter blocks into two words with the same meaning?

1 CE PR ER DE NT OP

2 CE AL ECI SP OI CH

3 TA KER NIT OR RE JA CA

4 OT NT PI SP OI NP

5 TAN TU ON RO EO IMP SP US MP

Wordsearch

How quickly can you find the five themed words in each grid?

RAIN

Y	L	E	V	P	U	H
Z	S	L	E	E	T	A
D	W	Z	S	A	Q	I
O	M	Z	B	N	S	L
R	C	I	I	F	O	H
K	J	R	N	T	G	W
X	E	D	T	S	I	M

SHOWER

K	A	S	P	X	Z	Y
F	P	H	C	A	S	U
L	H	A	F	O	O	L
I	W	M	D	H	M	S
B	O	P	Q	C	L	V
S	P	O	N	G	E	R
J	E	O	T	N	G	G

SHINE

N	P	B	U	F	F	V
A	V	O	N	G	A	E
E	B	T	L	R	P	M
L	D	J	N	I	Q	S
C	F	I	W	Z	S	R
X	S	A	H	E	I	H
H	L	C	O	Y	W	P

Vowel Play

Can you replace the missing vowels to complete these one-word TV shows?

1 DCTRS

2 SPKS

3 CST

4 HSTL

5 NWSNGHT

6 CSLTY

7 MRS

8 LST

9 PNRM

10 CNTDWN

Three in One

The three parts of each clue lead to the same answer word. Can you solve any before you reach the third part?

1 Scratch • Film music • Twenty

2 Carry • Suffer • Ursine creature

3 Song • Set (down) • Non-clergy

4 Golf stroke • Ambition
• Take the wheel

5 Chute • Hair clip • Slip

WORKOUT 29

Missing Link

The three words in each clue have a fourth word in common, and that's your answer. For example, the clue 'Moon • Navy • Royal' gives the answer BLUE (blue moon, navy blue, royal blue). Write each answer in the grid, and the shaded column will reveal a game.

1 Awake • Eyed • Open
2 Dog • Fish • Turn
3 Child • Intensive • Worn
4 Bun • Chair • Salts
5 Acid • Drive • Tube

1			
2			
3			
4			
5			

Codewords

If **FLAG=1234** and **IRON=5678**, how quickly can you work out these golf words? You should identify more letters as you go along.

1 9 3 4 2 9
2 10 7 2 9
3 11 3 2 2
4 11 5 6 12 5 9
5 13 7 7 12
6 13 9 12 4 9

Mind the Gap

Can you complete the five words in each set by adding the same three-letter word? For example OUR in HLY, VIG, FTH (hourly, vigour, fourth), and so on.

1 IMUS PARA PITE CARED CRUMS

2 ADD BEF FLT FST MISH

3 LER FISH SLE POCK GLEN

4 RED GUS DECT PERCTORY PRODITY

5 ITAL PROY CARAN INENT PEREE

Mini Jigsaw

Fit the pieces in the grid to spell out a colour in each row.

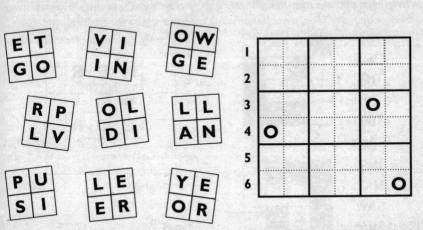

Killer Sudoku

TIME

The normal rules of Sudoku apply. Place a digit from 1-9 in each empty square so that each row, column and 3x3 block contains all the digits from 1-9. In addition, the digits in each inner shape (marked by dots) must add up to the number in the top corner of that box. No digit can be repeated within an inner shape.

WORKOUT 31

Mini Fit

Which one of the listed words won't fit in each of these mini grids?

HIT
OPT
THY
TIP
TOY

IMP
MAT
SAW
SUM
TWO

BELT
BOTH
LATE
TUBE
TUTU

DARE
DEAF
DENT
FAIR
FRET

Word Builder TIME

Using the nine letters provided, can you answer these clues? Every answer must include the highlighted letter C. What source of music uses all nine letters?

5 Letters
Instruct
Frighten
Tedious job
Crate
Bedlam
Pursue

6 Letters
Look (for)
Thespians
Type of sugar
Bodice

7 Letters
More vulgar
Portable lights
Drinks mat
Toxophilites

8 Letters
Makers
Energy-releasing devices

Splits

Can you rearrange each of these sets of letter blocks into a word? (As a bonus, you should spot a link between each word once correctly rearranged. What is the link?)

1 NE POR PI CU

2 DI NE ST SHO

3 ATE OK BO PL

4 ION AN MP CO

5 UG ERS GL SM

Memory Jog

You have two minutes to study the list of twenty words. Then give yourself another two minutes to write as many as you can recall on a separate piece of paper.

COLOUR	DOWNPOUR	FAN	OPENLY
BLANK	AFFABLE	POSTCARD	SPREAD
SPINE	WONDERMENT	FORK	COSTUME
COLLECT	ENVELOPE	CABLE	VOCAL
SPEEDILY	SHOWER	HOARSE	STICK

Pairs

Pair off 24 of the listed words to form twelve "double-barrelled" words and rearrange the letters of the two words left over to reveal **a fruit**.

BANK	DIVING	OPENER
BISCUIT	FIRE	PONY
BOARD	HOLIDAY	RACKET
BOTTLE	INSURANCE	SKIN
CAMP	LACE	SQUASH
CHEESE	LEANT	STOP
CLAIM	LEMON	TAIL
COCK	MOWER	TEA
CUP	NECK	

39

WORKOUT 33

Wordsearch

How quickly can you find the five themed words in each grid?

SPORTS

C	X	V	G	B	M	A
S	Y	E	K	C	O	H
I	U	C	Q	O	L	C
N	O	H	L	D	T	N
N	E	O	J	I	Z	Y
E	P	W	R	S	N	F
T	K	G	O	L	F	G

HERBS

B	O	L	L	I	D	T
H	R	M	X	L	H	V
F	E	L	I	Y	M	I
P	G	S	M	N	C	D
G	A	E	A	U	T	Z
B	N	J	N	E	T	K
R	O	Q	W	O	S	Y

Set Square   TIME

Place one each of the digits 1-9 in the grid to make the sums work. We've put in some of the numbers to start you off. Sums should be solved from left to right, or from top to bottom.

Cell Blocks   TIME

Fill the grid by drawing blocks along the gridlines. Each block must be square or rectangular and must contain the number of squares indicated by the digit inside it. Each block must contain only one digit.

40

Sudoku
TIME

Place a number in each empty square so that each row, each column and each 2x2 block contains all the numbers from 1-4.

1			4
	4	1	
	1	3	
3			1

	1	3	
3			1
2			3
	3	2	

3			4
	4	3	
	2	4	
4			2

Add Up
TIME

If the number in each circle is the sum of the two below it, how quickly can you figure out the top number? Try this one in your head, before writing anything down.

WORKOUT 35

Codeword

Can you crack the code and fill in the crossword grid? Each letter of the alphabet makes at least one appearance in the grid, and is represented by the same number wherever it appears. The four letters we've decoded should help you to identify other letters and words in the grid.

A B C D E F G H I J K L M N O P Q R S T U V W X Y Z

1	2 M	3 L	4	5	6	7	8	9	10	11	12	13
14	15	16	17	18	19	20	21 P	22	23	24	25	26 A

So Complete

Complete each trio of words with a common letter. The five letters will form the answer word. Where there is a choice of completing letter, you must decide which is needed.

SA_E	GOL_	LI_T	
PA_N	P_ER	CH_P	
WA_E	_EAR	RIN_	
AC_E	C_EF	_EAL	
S_EM	HAL_	FIS_	

Splits

 TIME

Can you rearrange each of these sets of letter blocks into a word?

1 HO PL USE AY   **4** IND RE MA ER

2 DE CO NT NFI   **5** ES TT LE OME

3 PE NG RI SHI

Pieceword

TIME

With the help of the Across clues only, can you fit the 16 pieces into their correct positions in the empty grid (which, when completed, will exhibit a symmetrical pattern)?

ACROSS

1 Twisted, warped

2 Popular myth

3 Substitute

4 Movie theatre

5 Dampening

6 Animal that suckles its young

7 *Away in a ___*, carol

8 High singing voice

9 To an excessive degree

10 Frosty atmosphere

11 Surround, put in a box

12 Slum district

43

WORKOUT 37

Letter Sequence **TIME**

What letter should replace the question mark in these sequences?

1 A, E, J, P, W, E, ?

2 L, I, J, F, G, B, ?

3 M, Q, M, I, M, U, M, E, ?

4 A, L, C, N, E, P, G, R, ?

5 Z, Y, W, T, P, K, ?

Mobile Code **TIME**

If **EXETER is 393837** on this phone keypad, what other British cities have the following numbers?

1 2284

2 4855

3 9675

4 53337

5 386333

6 2273433

Disavowel **TIME**

Can you complete this puzzle by adding all the vowels?
There are **13 As, 15 Es, 3 Is, 7 Os and 5 Us** in the puzzle.

	R		P			N		P	
		R		M			F		R		M
S	N			L			F	R		M	
		S	T			R		T		R
L		T		T	R		D			C
	N		S	T		Y		D		Y
S		R			S					
	R		N			N	D		R	
C		N	K		R		D	R		W
		T		L		B		G		
	S	S		F	Y		R			R

Fitword

TIME

When all of the listed words have been placed correctly in the grid, which one is left over?

4 letters

Dull

Echo

~~Eden~~

Mull

Note

Opus

Play

Semi

Shun

Tint

Urge

6 letters

Losing

Niggle

Tested

Traced

9 letters

Podginess

Scripting

| E | D | E | N |

Smart Sums

TIME

Try to avoid writing down anything but the final answers to these calculations… no counting on fingers allowed either!

1 Legs on a tripod x hours in two-and-a-half days

2 Hearts in a pack of cards + 'S's in POSSESSES

3 Syllables in CORIANDER x lives of a cat

4 Degrees in a circle ÷ consonants in WONDERFUL

5 Stripes on the US flag – number of Olympic rings

WORKOUT 39

Pathfinder TIME

Beginning with MARTIN,
and moving up, down, left or right,
one letter at a time, can you trace a
path of nineteen Saints?

L	E	A	D	M	T	I	N	D	A	L
D	I	N	A	A	R	E	B	R	X	E
A	V	E	S	T	E	R	N	A	A	N
D	I	R	E	H	B	A	Z	I	L	D
P	E	T	H	L	U	C	A	S	E	E
F	R	E	T	O	J	Y	M	A	P	R
R	A	E	W	S	E	H	O	U	O	U
C	N	M	O	L	P	T	E	L	L	I
I	R	T	H	O	H	H	N	I	D	S
S	A	B	N	E	L	E	N	C	E	B
G	A	B	R	I	E	L	A	T	N	E

Box Wise   TIME

Can you place the three-letter groups
in the boxes, so that neighbouring
boxes always make a six-letter word,
like PAR-DON or DON-ATE? We've
placed one group to start you off.

LEA

AIL	ENT	MUT	TON
BAL	ITY	SIL	VER
CAR	~~LEA~~	TAL	VES

Logical   TIME

Three horse-racing brothers won the top three places in the most recent
Grand Multinational steeplechase. From the information given, can you say
which brother rode which horse and in what position they finished?

**If Brendan wasn't the brother who rode Red Rose to victory,
and if Connor on Desert Dahlia finished immediately behind
Aidan, who rode Lilac Lilac and where did they finish?**

46

Set Square TIME

Place one each of the digits 1-9 in the grid to make the sums work. We've put in some of the numbers to start you off. Sums should be solved from left to right, or from top to bottom.

Sudoku TIME

Use your powers of reasoning to place numbers in the grid, so that each row, each column and each 3x3 block contains the numbers 1-9.

	6	4						
9			6					1
3		5	2			9		7
	7	2		5		1		
			8		3			
			1		5			8
	6	4		8			9	2
						3	1	
	4	3			7	8		

Staircase TIME

When the seven **Scottish clans** are correctly placed along the horizontal rows, the letters in the diagonal "staircase" will yield an eighth.

BARCLAY

CAMERON

LAMOND

MAXWELL

MENZIES

OGILVY

SCOTT

WORKOUT 41

Mini Fit

Which one of the listed words won't fit in each of these mini grids?

ANT
APE
MAT
NET
PET

PAL
PIP
PLY
PRY
RIP

BALL
LEAP
PLOT
TAPE
TELL

BABY
BANK
BLOB
BLUR
NEON

Wordsearch

Hidden in this wordsearch grid are fifteen words that follow red.

L	K	L	R	T	F	L	A	G
Q	A	E	V	L	N	C	X	D
H	E	R	R	I	N	G	E	L
A	F	R	I	W	E	D	Y	I
W	N	I	C	M	N	P	E	G
P	B	U	G	A	D	Y	A	H
S	T	Q	H	U	R	A	H	T
S	A	S	J	L	H	P	M	S
D	E	D	O	O	L	B	E	P
G	M	A	T	D	Z	O	A	T
R	E	P	P	E	P	C	E	I

Scramble

What dogs can be made from each of these sets of scrambled letters?

1 ROB EX
2 EEL BAG
3 LOOPED
4 PROTEIN
5 WITH PEP
6 HER CURL
7 ANT ALIAS
8 SEEK PINE

Niners

Form four nine-letter words using all twelve listed "syllables" (without altering the order of the letters in each "syllable"). Then enter them in the grid in the right order to reveal **daybreak** reading down the **left-hand** column.

AND	ARC	COU
DIS	ECT	HIT
HST	IAN	NOR
RSE	WEG	WIT

Memory Jog

Spend two minutes memorising this list of twenty words, then see how many of them you can recall on a separate piece of paper in another two minutes.

COW	TASTE	MESSAGE	ANGRY	PAPER
SKEWER	KEYS	YELLOW	FROG	PIANO
CANDLE	SEVEN	FIZZ	PEACH	SPOON
FINGER	TALK	SHINE	CHAIR	PEANUT

Kakuro

Simple addition and a bit of logical thinking will solve this one. You must write a digit in each white square so that the digits in each across section add up to the total in the triangle to the left, and the digits in each column add up to the total in the triangle above. 1-9 are the only digits to use and, although you may find a digit repeated in a row, it must not be repeated in the same section. We've solved one section for you.

49

WORKOUT 43

Arroword

Just follow the arrows to write your answers in the grid. A handful of anagram clues will get you thinking differently.

Genuine ▼	Go backwards ▼	▼	Large monkey ▼	▼	Mad with worry ▼	▼	Word of farewell ▼	▼
►								
Ecological political group (5,5) ►	Chimney deposit	RITE (anag)		___ Kourni-kova, tennis player		Consume (medicine)		
		▼		▼	TAN (anag) ►		▼	Went in front
STEER (anag) ►	From the East ►							▼
►			Greek goddess of victory ►					
Hangman's loop ►	Resembling a series of steps							

Initials

If **ITHOTN** (Oscar-winning fil*m*) *is*
IN THE HEAT OF THE NIGHT, what
do these initials represent?

1 KOTG (Park notice)

2 JATB (Pantomime)

3 MHMLW (Proverb)

4 TPOTO (Musical)

5 BCATSK (Western)

Number Sequence

What number should come
next in these sequences?

1 1, 2, 5, 10, 17, ?

2 100, 90, 81, 73, 66, ?

3 5, 10, 9, 18, 17, ?

4 1, 2, 5, 14, 41, ?

5 1, 2, 5, 10, 20, 50, ?

Dominoes

Solve the clues then write the six-letter answers into the dominoes. You must work out whether each word fits in clockwise or anticlockwise, so that the connecting letters of the dominoes all match up.

1 ___ Bear, cartoon bear from Nutwood

2 ___ Daley, George Cole's character in *Minder*

3 ___ *the Tank Engine*

4 *Shameless* actress, ___ Peake

5 ___ Woodward, wife of Paul Newman

6 ___ of Arimathea, biblical character

Mobile Code

If RED is 733 on this phone keypad, what colours have the following numbers?

1 2583

2 4653

3 7465

4 47336

5 787753

Four by Four

How quickly can you solve this mini crossword?

ACROSS

1 Prepare food

5 Fairy tale's second word?

6 Throw off track

7 Run away

DOWN

1 End of a sleeve

2 Milk-white gem

3 Seep out

4 Joint in the leg

WORKOUT 45

Fare's Fair

TIME

Find two words of the same sound but different spelling to satisfy each two-element clue, then decide which of the pair goes where in the grid to discover **a clergyman or chess piece**, reading down the arrowed column.

Young swan's ring

Flatfish's position

Fragrance dispatched

Purchaser of cattle-shed

Occasion for herb

Grieve early in the day

Futoshiki

TIME

Fill the blank squares so that each row and column contains all the numbers 1, 2 and 3. Use the given numbers and the symbols that tell you if the number in the square is larger (>) or smaller (<) than the number next to it.

Staircase

TIME

When the seven **foods** are correctly placed along the horizontal rows, the letters in the diagonal "staircase" will yield an eighth.

BUTTER

CEREAL

HOBNOB

HONEY

KEBAB

RAVIOLI

SAUSAGE

Mini Jigsaw

Fit the pieces in the grid to spell out a vegetable in each row.

Killer Sudoku

The normal rules of Sudoku apply. Place a digit from 1-9 in each empty square so that each row, column and 3x3 block contains all the digits from 1-9. In addition, the digits in each inner shape (marked by dots) must add up to the number in the top corner of that box. No digit can be repeated within an inner shape.

Sudoku TIME

Place a number in each empty square so that each row, each column and each 2x2 block contains all the numbers from 1-4.

	1	2	
4			3
	3	4	
1			2

	1		
4		2	
	2		3
		1	

	1		2
	4		3
	2		1
	3		4

Word Builder TIME

Using the nine letters provided, can you answer these clues? Every answer must include the highlighted letter C. What authority figure uses all nine letters?

P	E	A
O	C	L
N	I	M

5 Letters
Kayak
Desert animal
Contagious fear
Ground-up beef
Spotless
Edible nut

6 Letters
Sketching tool
Popular edible fish
Picture house
Wages

7 Letters
Positioned correctly (2,5)
Big-billed bird

8 Letters
Grumble

Alpha-Fit

Each of the 26 letters of the alphabet appears once in this crossword.

ACROSS
- **3** Changing residence (6)
- **5** Sounds like a duck (6)
- **7** Soft, gentle breeze (6)

DOWN
- **1** People (4)
- **2** Three-cornered sail (3)
- **4** Polished (5)
- **6** Pig's enclosure (3)

A	B	C	D	E	F	G	H	I	J	K	L	M
N	O	P	Q	R	S	T	U	V	W	X	Y	Z

Six Pack

Can you place digits in the empty triangles, so that the numbers in each hexagon add up to 25? Only single digits between 1 and 9 can be used, and no two digits in any hexagon may be the same.

Spot the Sum

In each of these boxes, one of the numbers is the sum of two others. Can you spot the sum?

1
7 32 20 1 9
4 15 34 22

2
33 18 5 12 29
37 11 3 31

3
24 12 4 37 18
30 9 29 23

4
6 19 39 15 29
8 35 26 30

WORKOUT 49

Elimination

All but two of the listed words fall into one of the four categories.
Put these leftover words together, and what phrase do they make?

CATEGORIES Musical instruments • Words preceding PIECE (eg Two) • Words without vowels • Reptiles

Myrrh	Square	Conversation	Turtle	Lynx	Master
Anaconda	Triangle	Bassoon	Meal	Viola	Iguana
Cymbals	Why	Crypt	Party	Hair	
Time	Cobra	Cornet	Alligator	Rhythm	

Logical

How quickly can you figure out what's what?

Implausible though it seems, three students have a rota of
household chores for Monday, Tuesday and Wednesday.
If Andrew's task is on Tuesday, but is not the ironing, and
the dusting is carried out later in the week than Brian's
gardening, what does Colin do and on which day?

Cell Blocks

TIME

Fill the grid by drawing blocks along the
gridlines. Each block must be square or
rectangular and must contain the number
of squares indicated by the digit inside it.
Each block must contain only one digit.

	3			2	
2					
4		9			
					6
	5				
2		3			

Splits

Can you rearrange each of these sets of letter blocks into a word?

1 GA LI TOR AL   **4** DE RM MA ALA

2 HO LOP NE XY   **5** NTI TE AL PO

3 PER ND SA PA

Shape Up

Can you arrange these five-letter shapes into their correct positions in the grid so that ten **surnames of film actresses** read down the columns?

WORKOUT 53

Two of a Kind TIME

Can you sort each set of letter blocks into two words with the same meaning?

1 AN SA AM SE OR IL
2 BIT RB FO OHI ID PR
3 NJ MAG ER CO AN ICI UR
4 EE PE ERS SU OV SE RVI
5 FE IAN ARD DE ER GU ND

Codewords TIME

If HOE=123 and PATH=4561, how quickly can you work out these items found in the garden? You should identify more letters as you go along.

1 4 3 5 6
2 4 2 6 5 6 2
3 7 1 2 2 6 7
4 4 3 6 5 8
5 5 4 4 8 3

Star Turn TIME

Which numbered photograph has been taken?

60

Fitword

TIME

When all of the listed words have been placed correctly in the grid, which one is left over?

3 letters

Dim
Eye
Icy
Irk
Lie
Pro
Vet
War

4 letters

Dole
Etch

5 letters

Emery
Heady
Huffy
Naval
Renal
~~Rigid~~

Tikka
Wiper

7 letters

Furlong
Seeming
Tactile

8 letters

Regulate
Sightsee

(Grid contains the word **R I G I D**)

Set Square

TIME

Place one each of the digits 1-9 in the grid to make the sums work. We've put in some of the numbers to start you off. Sums should be solved from left to right, or from top to bottom.

6	÷		+		= 11
+		+		−	
	−	4	+		= 6
−		×		÷	
	−		×		= 14

= 10   = 18   = 1

WORKOUT 55

Pathfinder

Beginning with CHICORY, and moving up, down, left or right, one letter at a time, can you trace a path of eighteen herbs?

C	H	I	S	R	O	S	E	M	A	R
S	E	V	E	E	N	N	E	I	S	Y
A	V	R	R	L	E	G	F	L	A	C
E	G	A	A	T	G	A	I	C	B	H
L	O	C	H	I	A	R	L	L	I	E
Y	N	O	R	C	S	M	O	C	V	R
A	A	G	E	O	R	A	R	R	E	D
B	N	O	Y	R	O	J	I	V	E	N
E	M	M	C	M	A	R	A	A	E	L
H	Y	I	O	R	E	D	N	L	Y	S
T	T	N	M	F	R	E	Y	P	A	R

Memory Jog

Spend two minutes memorising this list of twenty words, then see how many of them you can recall on a separate piece of paper in another two minutes.

SUITCASE	TREE	SIMPLE	CHANGE
MOUTH	WINDOW	TOWARDS	SHADE
SHIRT	JUMP	KETTLE	TAXI
COLD	SCISSORS	CARRY	IDEA
EARRING	FEATHER	MILK	GRASS

Pyramid

Each answer except the first uses all the letters – usually in a different order – from the previous answer plus one extra letter.

1 Abbreviation for "King"
2 Egyptian sun god
3 Epoch
4 Attention
5 Provide food
6 Hypnotic state
7 Sure
8 Metal container
9 Wrongdoer

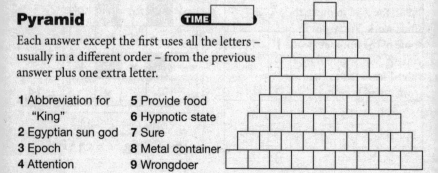

Mind the Gap

TIME

Can you place a different three-letter word in the spaces of each row to complete the seven-letter word? Do it correctly, and the shaded letters should spell out a musical instrument.

V	A				C	Y
G	O	R				A
C	A	B				E
A	C				A	T
E	C				S	E
T				K	L	E
E	A	R				R
S				C	I	L

Sudoku

TIME

Use your powers of reasoning to place numbers in the grid, so that each row, each column and each 3x3 block contains the numbers 1-9.

								3
			5					
5			4	1	9			
		9		8	4	1		
	5	1	2		6	7		
		2		3		6	9	
	1		3	7	8			
8	6	7		4				
	2				8			

Three in One

TIME

The three parts of each clue lead to the same answer word. Can you solve any before you reach the third part?

1 Just • Carnival • Blonde

2 Force • Golf stroke • Go by car

3 Cheek • Narrow opening • Body part

4 Depressed • Snooker ball • Sapphire colour

5 Divide • Section • Role

WORKOUT 57

Mini Fit

Which one of the listed words won't fit in each of these mini grids?

HAS
PAW
SIP
SKI
WHY

AXE
COD
COX
CUB
EBB

DONE
LAID
LINE
PLEA
SLIP

DEER
DROP
PRAM
STEM
TEST

Wordsearch TIME

Hidden in this wordsearch grid are fifteen types of deer.

A	N	T	E	L	O	P	E	K
A	C	R	F	S	D	S	L	T
Z	O	A	H	P	N	E	L	R
E	W	D	R	R	V	O	E	W
N	Z	O	U	I	B	J	Z	R
G	P	E	K	N	B	W	A	I
C	A	C	Y	G	G	O	G	J
Q	U	T	U	B	G	L	U	X
B	Q	H	S	O	M	L	I	L
T	R	A	H	K	D	A	T	K
M	O	O	S	E	E	F	F	C

Vowel Play

Can you replace the missing vowels to complete the names of these insects?

1 M T H
2 M S Q T
3 M D G
4 B T L
5 L C S T

6 T R M T
7 G N T
8 C C D
9 R W G
10 P H D

64

Smart Sums

Try to avoid writing down anything but the final answers to these calculations... and resist the temptation to count on your fingers!

1 Sides of a square x Lives of a cat

2 Letters of the alphabet + Days in the week

3 Degrees in a right angle ÷ Number of Is in LIAISING

4 Syllables in COSMOPOLITAN + Wives of Henry VIII

5 Legs on a spider – Vowels in TREAD

Mind the Gap

Can you complete the five words in each set by adding the same three-letter word? For example OUR in HLY, VIG, FTH (hourly, vigour, fourth), and so on.

1 PLD MEN BRLET PLBO ADJNT   4 HY COLL PIER MAROD DISHST

2 PI CHES FSAM CTED CUTES   5 BOR AIST ZIR ANAMA FURST

3 HOG PIG SACH OION SSTER

Kakuro

Simple addition and a bit of logical thinking will solve this one. You must write a digit in each white square so that the digits in each across section add up to the total in the triangle to the left, and the digits in each column add up to the total in the triangle above. 1-9 are the only digits to use and, although you may find a digit repeated in a row, it must not be repeated in the same section. We've solved one section for you.

	4	3		20	6	23	8			
4			13							
			6						12	16
45										
		19					17		8	9

WORKOUT 59

Arroword

Just follow the arrows to write your answers in the grid. A handful of anagram clues will get you thinking differently.

Narrow-mindedness ▼ / Air bed	Flat kitchen surface ▼	Language of South Africa ▼	Tummy muscles ▼	DAN (anag) ▼	▼
▶		Of the city ▶			
Refuse admittance to (4,3)	Dove's call	Norway's capital	STAB (anag)	RANG (anag)	
▶	▼	▼	▼ Gunk	▼ Idiot	▼
Little children ▶		Taj Mahal city	▼		▼
▶		Constrictor snakes			
Dribble	Toxins ▶				

Futoshiki

Fill the blank squares so that each row and column contains all the numbers 1, 2 and 3. Use the given numbers and the symbols that tell you if the number in the square is larger (>) or smaller (<) than the number next to it.

Small Change

Can you change one letter of each of these words to make five new words with a common theme?

1 SKIPPER • VANDAL • SLOG • MALE • BOUT
2 ACE • GRILL • HAMPER • SAD • CLASP
3 FOUL • NIFTY • NICE • OWE • LIGHT
4 FUDGE • CHEW • SET • PIVOT • CLEAVER
5 PAIN • SLOWER • SNOB • HALL • SLEEP

Number Jig

Which one of the listed numbers won't fit in each of these mini grids?

364
382
383
423
673

169
257
297
591
927

4825
5738
5743
7352
8375

2114
4162
4461
4661
6412

Codewords

If **HORSE=12345** and **SNAKE=46785**, how quickly can you work out these creatures? You should identify another letter as you go along.

1 156

2 1735

3 29953

4 49279

5 123659

Four by Four ⏱TIME

How quickly can you solve this mini crossword?

ACROSS

1 Soulful dance music
5 Zone, region
6 Effigy of a god
7 Mystic symbol

DOWN

1 Morally just
2 Official language of Pakistan
3 Noble gas
4 Dark green leafy vegetable

WORKOUT 61

In and Out

Without changing the order of the letters, add or remove one letter each time to leave a (different) new complete word and put the added or removed letters in their respective boxes to find **a fictional US lawyer played by Raymond Burr in a famous TV series** reading down the boxes.

SPORT	
CHAT	
CHAT	
THERM	
ERIE	

CAP	
WHEAT	
ROUSE	
CURSE	
CHANT	

Four by Four

How quickly can you solve this mini crossword?

1	2	3	4
5			
6			
7			

ACROSS
1 Bundle of hay
5 Leave the stage
6 Smart ___, wise guy
7 Fishing-net material

DOWN
1 Roof support
2 Rod joining two wheels
3 Fibs
4 Engrave

Splits

Can you rearrange each of these sets of letter blocks into a word?

1 CL LM FI ING

2 RVI TE IN EW

3 RE FU TU RNI

4 IRS AY HA PR

5 OI RQU TU SE

Mini Jigsaw

Fit the pieces in the grid to spell out a country in each row.

Killer Sudoku

The normal rules of Sudoku apply. Place a digit from 1-9 in each empty square so that each row, column and 3x3 block contains all the digits from 1-9. In addition, the digits in each inner shape (marked by dots) must add up to the number in the top corner of that box. No digit can be repeated within an inner shape.

WORKOUT 63

Initials TIME

If ITHOTN (Oscar-winning film) is *IN THE HEAT OF THE NIGHT*, what do these initials represent?

1 HAT (Cake decoration)

2 KUA (Sitcom)

3 AYLT (Elvis song)

4 ROTLA (Harrison Ford film)

5 BIACS (Clumsy person)

Missing Link TIME

The three words in each clue have a fourth word in common, and that's your answer. For example, the clue 'Moon • Navy • Royal' gives the answer BLUE (blue moon, navy blue, royal blue). Write each answer in the grid, and the shaded column will reveal a constellation.

1 Heat • Length • Mexican

2 Door • File • Thumb

3 Birth • Down • Question

4 Jump • Knee • Light

5 Bare • Step • Stool

Fix Six TIME

The six **rivers** listed will fit into this pattern of six adjoining hexagons. All are entered clockwise from a triangle to be discovered. Adjoining triangles always contain the same letter. The **B** gives you a start.

COQUET   KENNET

DANUBE   THAMES

GANGES   TIGRIS

Wild Words

What well-known phrases and expressions are suggested by these word pictures?

1 **ARREST**
 YOU'RE

3 **HACASHND**

2 EVER EVER
 EVER EVER

4 **0,2,3,4,5**

Elimination

All but two of the listed words fall into one of the four categories.
Put these leftover words together, and what new phrase do they make?

CATEGORIES Gemstones • Words meaning DRAW • Words following BREAD (eg Bin) •
Parts of the face

Brow	Line	Raffle	Crumb	Sauce	Sketch
Pull	Band	Jade	Attract	Amber	Lip
Jet	Diamond	Chin	Opal	Brass	
Nose	Winner	Stick	Tie	Cheek	

Copycats

Choose the answer that best copies the pattern.

LEFT is to RIGHT as RIGHT is to: Correct • Angle • Proper • Wrong • Hand

HARE is to LEVERET as EEL is to: Jelly • Elver • Heifer • Snake • Fish

SHAPE is to TRIANGLE as PIANO is to: Key • Tune • Pedal • Heavy • Upright

8361 is to 1863 as 2794 is to: 4297 • 7924 • 4279 • 7249 • 7429

VEGETARIAN is to HAM as VEGAN is to: Milk • Apple • Peanut • Rice • Lentil

WORKOUT 65

Wordsearch

How quickly can you find the five themed words in each grid?

FRUIT

A	N	A	N	A	B	P
O	P	Y	I	H	A	P
I	R	R	C	W	A	N
U	C	A	I	P	I	E
B	E	L	A	C	G	K
P	W	Y	X	S	O	V
J	A	H	D	K	M	T

GALLERY

B	A	R	L	S	E	S
H	K	O	Q	U	F	A
M	J	T	T	R	A	V
U	C	A	Y	G	R	N
E	T	R	Z	X	V	A
S	W	U	I	O	P	C
P	I	C	T	U	R	E

Vowel Play

Can you replace the missing vowels to complete the names of these fabrics?

1 SLK   4 RYN   7 PLD   10 SD

2 DNM   5 TWD   8 LNN

3 WL   6 PSLY   9 NGR

Cell Blocks

Fill the grid by drawing blocks along the gridlines. Each block must be square or rectangular and must contain the number of squares indicated by the digit inside it. Each block must contain only one digit.

Sudoku TIME

Place a number in each empty square so that each row, each column and each 2x2 block contains all the numbers from 1-4.

Add Up TIME

If the number in each circle is the sum of the two below it, how quickly can you figure out the top number? Try this one in your head, before writing anything down.

A B C D E F G H I J K L M N O P Q R S T U V W X Y Z

Codeword

Can you crack the code and fill in the crossword grid? Each letter of the alphabet makes at least one appearance in the grid, and is represented by the same number wherever it appears. The four letters we've decoded should help you to identify other letters and words in the grid.

Spot the Sum

In each of these boxes, one of the numbers is the sum of two others. Can you spot the sum?

1

```
  7   32    20    1    9
    4   15   34     22
```

2

```
  33   18    5    12   29
    37   11    3     31
```

3

```
  24   12    4    37   18
    30    9   29     23
```

4

```
  6   19    39   15   29
    8    35    26    30
```

Scramble

What countries can be made from each of these sets of scrambled letters?

1 PURE

2 WEALS

3 OLD PAN

4 MEG RYAN

5 REGALIA

6 A THIN LAD

7 ABSORB AD

8 MOON RACE

Tennis Match

Which numbered photograph has been taken?

WORKOUT 69

Futoshiki

Fill the blank squares so that each row and column contains all the numbers 1, 2, 3 and 4. Use the given numbers and the symbols that tell you if the number in the square is larger (>) or smaller (<) than the number next to it.

Letter Sequence

What letter should replace the question-mark in these sequences?

1 A, D, G, J, ?

2 X, V, T, R, ?

3 Y, ?, P, M, K

4 P, D, ?, E, N, F, M

5 J, F, M, A, M, J, ?

Disavowel

Can you complete this puzzle by adding all the vowels?
There are **13 As, 16 Es, 7 Is, 6 Os and 1 U** in the puzzle.

R		D		S	H		H		C	K
	R		M			B		R		N
S		M	P	L			P		R	
P			L		D		P	L		
	S		Y			C				D
D		J			T		N			
	K		P				S			R
C		C		D				T		
	N	K	S		L		T	H		L
L			T	H		R			W	
		L						R	L	S

Fitword

TIME

When all of the listed words have been placed correctly in the grid, which one is left over?

3 letters
Chi
Cob
Eat
Ops
Out
Rig
Tod

4 letters
Abut
Debt
Sigh
Sour

5 letters
~~Again~~
Bulge
Heaps

Revel
Tread
Vying

7 letters
Circled
Origami

8 letters
Fretting
Peculiar

Set Square

TIME

Place one each of the digits 1-9 in the grid to make the sums work. We've put in some of the numbers to start you off. Sums should be solved from left to right, or from top to bottom.

9	+		÷		= 5
−		×		+	
	×		−	1	= 9
+		−		×	
	+		−		= 11
=		=		=	
14		22		16	

WORKOUT 71

Pathfinder TIME

Beginning with WOOD, and moving up, down, left or right, one letter at a time, can you trace a path of twenty-two golfing words?

E	A	E	G	G	E	R	Y	D	E	R
S	G	L	O	D	E	W	G	A	L	C
S	O	R	L	F	B	I	R	D	F	U
O	U	D	R	A	U	O	R	I	E	P
R	G	O	R	Z	N	R	E	K	A	C
T	H	F	E	A	D	E	L	N	D	D
A	B	L	A	H	F	A	O	U	B	Y
D	O	O	[W]	Y	A	I	H	G	T	I
G	E	L	L	A	W	R	I	N	C	P
R	R	B	M	B	H	A	W	S	H	P
E	E	N	U	A	G	N	D	I	C	A

Memory Jog

You have two minutes to study the list of twenty words. Then give yourself another two minutes to write as many of the words as you can recall on a separate piece of paper.

FREE	SNAIL	SAUNA	SWIM	ECHO
CARPET	LETTER	FENCE	WINE	ZERO
KEYBOARD	PALM	BABY	MAYBE	EARWAX
JAM	DREAM	BANANA	COWBOY	INK

Pairs TIME

Pair off 24 of the listed words to form twelve "double-barrelled" words and rearrange the letters of the two words left over to reveal **a pop group or a position of desperate difficulty**.

BLACK	BREAKFAST	CLOTH	CYCLIST	DRESSING
DRIVING	FEED	FRENCH	HEAD	MARKET
PARTY	SPOON	START	TIRED	
BREAK	CHANNEL	COFFEE	DAY	
ENGLISH	FOUR	GREEN	LICENCE	
SCHOOL	STAIRS	TABLE	TRICK	

Honeycomb

Write the six-letter answers clockwise round their respective cell-numbers, starting at the arrowed cell. On completion, you will find that the unclued answers (10 and 11) will reveal **a former Tory Chancellor of the Exchequer**.

1 Distant (3,3)

2 Captor's demand

3 Go without food

4 Have in mind

5 Leisurely country walk

6 Ill-will

7 Frequently encountered

8 He shrinks from danger

9 Strand of pasta in chicken soup

Sudoku

Use your powers of reasoning to place numbers in the grid, so that each row, each column and each 3x3 block contains the numbers 1-9.

			9					8
				8	5	4		
		8	2	3				9
	7	1				9	6	
			6	1	2			
4	6					1	8	
1				9	6	7		
		5	7	4				
8					3			

Mobile Code

If MAPLE is 62753 on this phone keypad, what trees have the following numbers?

1	2 ABC	3 DEF
4 GHI	5 JKL	6 MNO
7 PQRS	8 TUV	9 WXYZ
*	0	#

1 625

2 7463

3 23327

4 24724

5 945569

6 222242

WORKOUT 73

Word Builder TIME

Using the nine letters provided, can you answer these clues? Every answer must include the highlighted letter R. What spread uses all nine letters?

G	I	A
R	R	M
E	A	N

5 Letters
Rule over a country
Dirt
Sports stadium
Colliery worker
Irate emotion
Single piece of sand

6 Letters
European language
Stay behind
Yacht harbour
Italian designer label
Page border
Optical illusion

7 Letters
Person in charge
Item of jewellery

8 Letters
Wedding

Wordsearch TIME

Hidden in this wordsearch grid are fifteen cooking methods.

P	Z	U	R	V	A	Y	Q	S
R	B	A	K	O	R	Y	M	A
T	H	A	H	F	A	P	J	U
C	S	B	R	A	I	S	E	T
W	H	A	C	B	R	F	T	E
E	C	R	O	S	E	K	A	B
T	A	W	D	T	M	C	T	G
S	O	D	D	I	M	C	U	B
M	P	O	L	E	I	L	O	E
J	M	A	E	T	S	I	N	B
G	R	I	L	L	L	G	X	W

Opposites Attract TIME

Can you sort each set of letter blocks into two words with opposite meanings?

1 UR SWE SO ET

2 HT OSE LO TIG

3 RO AK NG ST WE

4 CE IT RAN EX ENT

5 VE PE AP EX CHE NSI

Memory Quiz

Here's a quiz to see how much attention you're really
paying to your surroundings. No peeping!

1 What colour are the benches in the House of Commons?

2 How many sides has a twenty pence coin?

3 Supercede – is that the correct spelling?

4 In which hand does the Statue of Liberty hold the torch?

5 What is the colour of fire exit signs in the UK?

6 On a keyboard, is the V or B further left?

Smart Sums

Try to avoid writing down anything but the final answers to
these calculations... no counting on fingers allowed either!

1 Letters in CAMSHAFT – Syllables in CARBURETTOR

2 Days in September ÷ Es in BEEKEEPER

3 Leaves on a lucky clover x Vowels in MOZAMBIQUE

4 Minutes in an hour – Consonants in POLYTHENE

5 Squares on a chessboard + Legs on a tripod

Kakuro

Simple addition and a bit of logical thinking will solve this one. You must write
a digit in each white square so that the digits in each across section add up to
the total in the triangle to the left, and the digits in each column add up to
the total in the triangle above. 1-9 are the only digits to use and, although you may
find a digit repeated in a row, it must not be repeated in the same section.
We've solved one section for you.

WORKOUT 75

Arroword

Just follow the arrows to write your answers in the grid. A handful of anagram clues will get you thinking differently.

(Of the night sky) twinkly ▼	Number in a duet ▼	Soil fertiliser ▼	▼	Pastry dish	▼	TREASON (anag)	— interest, personal stake
Haulage line (3-4) ►				▼		CLEAR (anag)	▼
Part of a curve	Pacify	Chop finely ►				▼	
►	▼	Scottish river	PALES (anag)				
Wireless ►		▼		Shabby odds and ends ►			
			Sleeper's grunt!				
► Jeremy __, talk-show host	Turn to liquid			Garnet colour ►			

Staircase

When the seven **composers** are correctly placed along the horizontal rows, the letters in the diagonal "staircase" will yield an eighth.

BRITTEN
DVORAK
ELGAR
GLINKA
MAHLER
ROSSINI
STRAUSS

Small Change

Can you change one letter of each of these words to make five new words with a common theme?

1 BARGE • BUG • VASE • CHOPPING • PASSIVE

2 PELMET • PULP • BAKE • RICE • MEDAL

3 GAMBLE • MATCH • WALL • STRUM • HIRE

4 STEAL • CORK • PEACH • DIMMER • PRY

Number Jig

Which one of the listed numbers won't fit in each of these mini grids?

259
752
792
799
925

123
133
217
371
721

4896
6884
6948
8496
9464

3517
3578
5131
8317
8573

Splits

Can you rearrange each of these sets of letter blocks into a word?

1 GE PA ID RTR
2 NG HI MET SO
3 ART QU LY ER
4 SE TH OR CAR
5 LE OZ MBO BA

Four by Four

How quickly can you solve this mini crossword?

1	2	3	4
5			
6			
7			

ACROSS

1 Suddenly run off
5 Neighbourhood
6 Harsh grating sound
7 Otherwise

DOWN

1 Starkers
2 Spoken test
3 Not as much
4 Record on video

WORKOUT 77

Niners

Form four nine-letter words using all twelve listed "syllables" (without altering the order of the letters in each "syllable"). Then enter them in the grid in the right order to reveal **a Scottish family group** reading down the **left-hand** column.

APA	CAL	CHE
ERI	ENT	LAB
MIS	NTH	NUM
RTM	TRY	YRI

All Fours

Fit the four listed words across the rows of the grid so that four more words read downwards.

AMEN

CORK

RILE

STYE

Box Wise

Can you place the three-letter groups in the boxes, so that neighbouring boxes always make a six-letter word, like PAR-DON or DON-ATE? We've placed one group to start you off.

BIL	FUL	LED	RAI
COU	GER	LET	SIN
FIL	LAD	~~LOW~~	THY

Mini Jigsaw

TIME

Fit the pieces in the grid to spell out a animal in each row.

Killer Sudoku

TIME

The normal rules of Sudoku apply. Place a digit from 1-9 in each empty square so that each row, column and 3x3 block contains all the digits from 1-9. In addition, the digits in each inner shape (marked by dots) must add up to the number in the top corner of that box. No digit can be repeated within an inner shape.

WORKOUT 79

Futoshiki TIME

Fill the blank squares so that each row and column contains all the numbers 1, 2 and 3. Use the given numbers and the symbols that tell you if the number in the square is larger (>) or smaller (<) than the number next to it.

Word Builder TIME

Using the nine letters provided, can you answer these clues? Every answer must include the highlighted letter N. What major port of SE Asia uses all nine letters?

R	I	E
O	N	P
S	A	G

5 Letters
Kitchen garment
Part of a fork
Sigh loudly
Backbone

6 Letters
Fruit
Take no notice of
Higher in rank
Racing bird
Clergyman
Persuade to take part (4,2)

7 Letters
Freeloader
Taking place outside (4-3)
Prehistoric period (4,3)
Extremely hot

8 Letters
Make preparations for

Fare's Fair

Find two words of the same sound but different spelling to satisfy each two-element clue, then decide which of the pair goes where in the grid to discover **the Christian name of Mr Marr, who presents BBC's** *Sunday AM*, reading down the arrowed column.

Painful tool

Trapped at judicial building

Moisture is about to arrive

Sheet of glass's dull ache

Lift up sunbeams

Team moaned

Splits

Can you rearrange each of these sets of letter blocks into a word?

1 WE UN AR DER

2 EN ER GRE EV

3 MU TY NI COM

4 LE ATH CS TI

5 RE NIA TU MI

Memory Jog

Give yourself two minutes to memorise this list of words – thirty this time! How many of them can you recall on a separate piece of paper in another two minutes?

PLIERS	CARAVAN	ARMCHAIR	CIDER	GUITAR	CIRCLE
BOX	GOAL	APRICOT	TRAIN	SHOE	HAPPY
PUZZLE	BRIDGE	SCHOOL	LEFT	TOFFEE	TOWEL
ANKLE	FAN	FUNNY	SAUCER	FLOOR	
STREAM	UNDER	MASCOT	JUST		
TYPE	GLITTER	LIZARD			

WORKOUT 81

Memory Jog

Spend two minutes memorising this list of twenty words, then see how many of them you can recall on a separate piece of paper.

MONKEYS	TALKING	SPRY	ROLL
THOUGHT	IDEA	SELL	QUILT
SONG	PASTY	WORLD	WAGGISH
LIVING	FLAVOUR	LIKEABLE	CAMP
WAGON	ACCENT	MYSELF	STARSHIP

Logical

Try solving this little logical problem in your head before putting pen to paper.

Tom, Dick and Harry are each planning their weekend camping trips to the Lake District, Peak District and Yorkshire Dales. The most important part of the planning was which luxury to take with them – brandy, chocolate or tea bags.

Dick planned his trip to the Peak District, and his luxury wasn't brandy. Tom's luxury was chocolate, and his trip wasn't to the Yorkshire Dales. Who went where and what was their luxury?

Cell Blocks

Fill the grid by drawing blocks along the gridlines. Each block must be square or rectangular and must contain the number of squares indicated by the digit inside it. Each block must contain only one digit.

Sudoku

Place a number in each empty
square so that each row, each
column and each 2x2 block
contains all the numbers from 1-4.

4			2
	2	4	
	4	3	
3			4

1			2
	2	1	
	1	3	
3			1

	3	4	
	1	3	
	4	2	
	2	1	

Wordsearch TIME

How quickly can you find the seven
themed words in each grid?

HORSE

P	Y	E	K	C	O	J
E	U	T	S	R	B	R
L	P	R	U	Z	E	E
D	J	O	R	T	W	I
D	E	T	N	I	N	N
A	A	A	C	H	T	S
S	C	J	U	M	P	S

CHEST

C	K	N	U	R	T	K
O	V	B	L	I	B	N
F	B	O	X	A	X	E
F	C	A	S	K	E	T
E	C	K	J	U	O	A
R	E	P	M	A	H	R
T	A	Q	E	T	M	C

NUT

L	W	P	A	G	X	A
I	A	E	P	V	L	J
Z	L	C	H	M	E	F
A	N	A	O	S	Z	B
R	S	N	W	Y	A	I
B	D	H	P	K	H	C
M	O	N	K	E	Y	Z

Codeword

Can you crack the code and fill in the crossword grid?
Each letter of the alphabet makes at least one appearance in the grid, and is represented by the same number wherever it appears. The four letters we've decoded should help you to identify other letters and words in the grid.

A B C Ø É F G H I J K L M N O P Q Ŕ S Ţ U V W X Y Z

1	2	3	4	5	6	7	8	9	10	11	12	13
14	15 D	16	17	18 T	19 E	20 R	21	22	23	24	25	26

So Complete

Complete each trio of words with a common letter. The five letters will form the answer word. Where there is a choice of completing letter, you must decide which is needed.

WIL_	WI_E	I_LE	
WA_N	W_EN	WEA_	
DE_R	MO_T	AL_S	
CA_E	_ORD	LEA_	
_EST	MA_E	SE_T	

Spot the Sum

TIME

In each of these boxes, one of the numbers is the sum of two others. Can you spot the sum?

Pieceword

TIME

With the help of the Across clues only, can you fit the 16 pieces into their correct positions in the empty grid (which, when completed, will exhibit a symmetrical pattern)?

ACROSS

1 Virtuous

2 Almost, approximately

3 Acclimatised

4 Baffling mystery

5 Crisp lustrous silk

6 Game played with an oval ball

7 Sludge

8 ___ colours, red, blue and yellow

9 Fairy cave

10 Criminal's lever

11 Take-off

12 Poem with fourteen lines

WORKOUT 85

Scramble TIME

The names of which high-street shops can be made from each of these sets of scrambled letters?

1 COT ME

2 NAVES

3 RUB NOT

4 RIVING

5 NICE LAD

6 HOT POPS (3,4)

7 REACH METRO

8 STOWS NEATER

Four by Four TIME

How quickly can you solve this mini crossword?

1	2	3	4
5			
6			
7			

ACROSS
1 Lionise
5 Crooked
6 Animal pen
7 Observed

DOWN
1 Shoe fastener
2 Absent
3 Strong desire
4 Colour-stained

Town to Town

Can you travel from **Harlech** to **Braemar** by removing or adding one letter at each stage from the definitions below, which are consequent anagrams?

1 ___ Weisz, star of *The Constant Gardener*

2 Distinct, not cloudy

3 Genuine

4 Historical age

5 Female horse

6 Traffic lights' "yellow"

7 Full-pitched cricket delivery bowled at the batsman's head

Fitword

TIME

When all of the listed words have been placed correctly in the grid, which one is left over?

3 letters
Ago
Ion

Piece
Pined
Spite

Tampered
Vagabond
War paint

4 letters
Ibis
Tidy

7 letters
Illness
Morello

9 letters
Balancing
Propelled

5 letters
Dregs

8 letters
~~Proposer~~
Scolding

P R O P O S E R

Six Pack

TIME

Can you place digits in the empty triangles, so that the numbers in each hexagon add up to 25? Only single digits between 1 and 9 can be used, and no two numbers in any hexagon may be the same.

WORKOUT 87

Pathfinder TIME

Beginning with *THE BOYFRIEND*, and moving up, down, left or right, one letter at a time, can you trace a path of fourteen musicals?

O	D	P	P	Y	R	G	N	N	O	I
O	A	I	O	P	A	M	I	K	E	L
N	G	N	O	K	L	A	I	R	H	T
G	I	S	L	H	A	H	R	I	T	Y
O	R	B	L	O	M	A	A	H	C	T
D	S	P	E	A	M	M	I	A	E	E
S	F	N	Y	M	E	A	M	G	W	S
D	U	N	F	A	C	C	I	R	E	E
O	T	O	T	O	G	A	H	T	A	S
O	H	I	N	M	N	D	C	H	E	B
W	E	E	M	A	E	I	R	F	Y	O

Soundalikes

Can you complete each of these sentences with two words that sound alike, but are spelled differently?

1 She ___ the ___ and improved version would work.
2 The walkers clambered over the ___ in some ___.
3 '___ be proud to walk you down the ___,' said the father to his daughter on her wedding day.
4 The fishmonger advised the body-builder to eat more ___ if he wanted bigger ___.

Copycats

Choose the answer that best copies the pattern.

FISH is to HERRING as BIRD is to: Tail • Feather • Fly • Duck • Beak

11 is to 121 as 13 is to: 169 • 213 • 131 • 193 • 129

CARE is to CASE as DALE is to: Dare • Dame • Dole • Pale • Date

DRUM is to STICK as VIOLIN is to: String • Peg • Bow • Fiddle • Pluck

Buzz Off

TIME

Which two pictures are identical?

Sudoku

TIME

Use your powers of reasoning to place numbers in the grid, so that each row, each column and each 3x3 block contains the numbers 1-9.

			2			3		7
			8		3	4	9	6
		3			9			1
6	3				4			
					6		8	
	5	9	3	1				
5	8							
	2			4				8
1	9	4				7		

Splits

TIME

Can you rearrange each of these sets of letter blocks into a word?

1 CON ED CE RN

2 NI MA ST CHI

3 UL AU BE TIF

4 VA BOU RD LE

5 AN PA TRY GE

WORKOUT 89

Dominoes

Solve the clues then write the six-letter answers into the dominoes. You must work out whether each word fits in clockwise or anticlockwise, so that the connecting letters of the dominoes all match up.

1 ___ Peacock, Claire's husband in *Coronation Street*
2 ___ Mouse, cartoon character
3 ___ Staunton, award-winning actress who played Vera Drake
4 The dog in *The Magic Roundabout*
5 ___ Gates, *Pop Idol* star
6 ___ Hussain, former cricket captain of England

Wordsearch TIME

Hidden in this wordsearch grid are fifteen cheeses.

Y	B	R	E	D	E	U	L	B
S	T	I	L	T	O	N	E	J
D	R	F	O	Y	P	D	Q	X
B	G	A	A	C	A	A	Z	U
E	R	E	D	M	R	R	R	H
W	U	L	U	D	M	E	G	J
K	Y	U	O	F	E	T	A	V
R	E	O	G	N	S	H	P	M
M	R	R	A	G	A	I	C	Y
T	E	P	N	Y	N	K	S	L
A	T	T	O	C	I	R	C	B

Futoshiki TIME

Fill the blank squares so that each row and column contains all the numbers 1, 2 and 3. Use the given numbers and the symbols that tell you if the number in the square is larger (>) or smaller (<) than the number next to it.

96

Smart Sums

Try to avoid writing down anything but the final answers to these calculations… and resist the temptation to count on your fingers!

1 Vowels in ALABASTER + ounces in 2lbs

2 Hours in March and May – days in January, June and July

3 Top number on a dartboard + usable squares on a draughts board

4 Syllables in CORONET x corners on 2 dice

5 5p pieces needed to make £2.55 – age you become eligible to vote

Small Change

Can you change one letter of each of these words to make five new words with a common theme?

1 SWAP • FRIDGE • MUMMY • POWER • WHISK

2 DAIRY • AMP • TRILL • ELK • PERT

3 BARE • ROOST • FRILL • STEM • POUCH

4 BEACON • DEAR • MERGER • BEAGLE • CASTOR

Kakuro

Simple addition and a bit of logical thinking will solve this one. You must write a digit in each white square so that the digits in each across section add up to the total in the triangle to the left, and the digits in each column add up to the total in the triangle above. 1-9 are the only digits to use and, although you may find a digit repeated in a row, it must not be repeated in the same section. We've solved one section for you.

WORKOUT 91

Arroword

Just follow the arrows to write your answers in the grid. A handful of anagram clues will get you thinking differently.

Noisy party ▼ / HOSE (anag)	Fiendish ▼	Deprive of life or vitality ▼	Mr Stallone's nickname ▼		Remains after burning ▼
►		Does nothing ►			
Heathen	Weapon	MODE (anag)	Village People hit (inits)		Rod with magical properties
►	▼	▼		Organ controlling balance ▼	▼ __ Moines, Iowa's capital ▼
NUDE (anag) ►			Fermented honey drink ►		
►			Bamboo stick ►		
In music, a double note ►	People lacking courage ►				

Vowel Play

Can you replace the missing vowels to complete the names of these sports?

1 J D
2 P L
3 R B C S
4 K R T
5 B X N G
6 D V N G
7 R G B Y
8 T N N S
9 R C H R Y
10 F T B L L

Two of a Kind

Can you sort each set of letter blocks into two words with the same meaning?

1 CO NU RY ENT NV NNE

2 DE NS TE ER BE CO LI RA ID

3 SU RE SH UP OT LT

4 FU NG IR UL MI EF

5 GI NG ER LA LI UG GG HT

Fix Six

The six **items of food** listed will fit into this pattern of six adjoining hexagons. All are entered clockwise from a triangle to be discovered. Adjoining triangles always contain the same letter. The **Q** gives you a start.

CANAPE	HUMMUS
CHEESE	QUICHE
HAGGIS	SALAMI

Mobile Code

If YORK is 9675 on this phone keypad, what county towns have the following numbers?

1 33729

2 87876

3 393837

4 4779424

5 8286866

Initials

If **ITHOTN** (Oscar-winning film) is *IN THE HEAT OF THE NIGHT*, what do these initials represent?

1 TVQ (Monarch's nickname)

2 TKAM (Classic US novel and film)

3 TWTIA (ABBA hit)

4 KHAC (Ealing comedy)

5 NABNALB (Proverb)

Mind the Gap

Can you place a well-known three-letter word in the spaces of each row to complete the seven-letter word? Do it correctly, and the shaded letters should spell out something to eat.

Four by Four

How quickly can you solve this mini crossword?

1	2	3	4
5			
6			
7			

ACROSS

1 Small ship
5 Arab prince
6 Yield (to another)
7 Joint of the leg

DOWN

1 At your ___ and call, at your service
2 Prophetic sign
3 Adviser
4 Plant with a trunk

Box Wise

Can you place the three-letter groups in the boxes, so that neighbouring boxes always make a six-letter word, like PAR-DON or DON-ATE? We've placed one group to start you off.

BAL	LIN	GEY	SAM
BIL	LOW	MAR	SER
LET	GER	PUR	~~VER~~

Mini Jigsaw

TIME

Fit the pieces in the grid to spell out a sport in each row.

| I | S |
| S | H |

| B | O |
| S | H |

| E | Y |
| N | G |

| C | K |
| I | I |

| N | G |
| T | Y |

| N | N |
| U | A |

| X | I |
| I | N |

| T | E |
| S | Q |

| H | O |
| S | K |

1					
2		H			
3					
4					H
5	H				
6					

Killer Sudoku

TIME

The normal rules of Sudoku apply. Place a digit from 1-9 in each empty square so that each row, column and 3x3 block contains all the digits from 1-9. In addition, the digits in each inner shape (marked by dots) must add up to the number in the top corner of that box. No digit can be repeated within an inner shape.

Killer Sudoku grid with cage clues: 23, 3, 14, 22, 14, 8, 8, 10, 16, 11, 17, 8, 4, 20, 12, 11, 7, 6, 16, 9, 6, 22, 20, 17, 8, 10, 16, 15, 13, 5, 14, 20

Word Builder TIME

Using the nine letters provided, can you answer these clues? Every answer must include the highlighted letter C. Which artisan uses all nine letters?

R	E	N
A	C	T
R	E	P

5 Letters
Lack of hostility
Mother-of-pearl
Put up
Frolic
Type of nut
Storage box

6 Letters
Of late
Professional life
Floor covering
Make
Middle
Drink of the gods

7 Letters
Row of houses
Perform again
Go over again

Number Jig TIME

Which one of the listed numbers won't fit in each of these mini grids?

689
768
879
897
987

327
352
435
478
528

5678
5768
6785
6857
8675

1212
2112
2123
3232
3322

In and Out

TIME

Without changing the order of the letters, add or remove one letter each time to leave a (different) new complete word and put the added or removed letters in their respective boxes to find **the envoy who was a hostage in Lebanon from 1987 until 1991** reading down the boxes.

SEAM		TON	
CRAM		TAUT	
TROUGH		DEAL	
SPRAIN		SLEIGHT	
TANS		CREATE	

Set Square

TIME

Place one each of the digits 1-9 in the grid to make the sums work. We've put in some of the numbers to start you off. Sums should be solved from left to right, or from top to bottom.

Elimination

TIME

All but two of the listed words fall into one of the four categories. Put these leftover words together, and what word do they make?

CATEGORIES Words following KEY (eg Signature) • Space • Types of pastry • London Underground lines

Board	Flaky	Meal	Note	Shortcrust	Choux
Planet	Star	Ring	Jubilee	Central	Moon
Circle	Bakerloo	Satellite	Orbit	Filo	
Pad	Puff	Northern	Stone	Whole	

WORKOUT 97

Wordsearch

How quickly can you find the seven themed words in each grid?

SUN ____

B	R	S	Y	T	O	F
J	A	E	H	T	A	B
I	W	G	W	I	K	E
L	I	R	T	O	N	H
L	N	O	E	Z	L	E
T	G	O	S	C	X	F
P	D	F	Y	A	D	S

____ MOON

O	L	Z	T	F	A	P
W	L	Y	S	D	G	A
E	U	W	E	N	V	P
H	F	U	V	N	M	E
U	L	C	R	J	O	R
B	F	L	A	H	B	H
N	I	T	H	Q	P	L

Splits

Can you rearrange each of these sets of letter blocks into a word?

1 RA MI BLE SE

2 ST HY CS ERI

3 TE AC HU PAR

4 ES TI AL SEN

5 ARB ST RD OA

Cell Blocks

Fill the grid by drawing blocks along the gridlines. Each block must be square or rectangular and must contain the number of squares indicated by the digit inside it. Each block must contain only one digit.

104

Sudoku

Place a number in each empty square so that each row, each column and each 2x2 block contains all the numbers from 1-4.

	1	2	
3			1
1			2
	3	1	

	4	1	
1			4
3			1
	1	3	

3			1
	1	3	
	4	1	
1			4

Add Up

If the number in each circle is the sum of the two below it, how quickly can you figure out the top number? Try this one in your head, before writing anything down.

105

WORKOUT 99

Codeword

Can you crack the code and fill in the crossword grid? Each letter of the alphabet makes at least one appearance in the grid, and is represented by the same number wherever it appears. The four letters we've decoded should help you to identify other letters and words in the grid.

A B C D E F G H I J K L M N O P Q R S T U V W X Y Z

1	2	3	4	5	6	7	8	9	10	11	12	13
						A		**I**		**P**		
14	15	16	17	18	19	20	21	22	23	24	25	26
									R			

Copycats

Choose the answer that best copies the pattern.

TIME

$1/_8$ **is to 0.125 as** $2/_5$ **is to:** 0.25 • 0.33 • 0.4 • 0.525 • 0.6

PANEL is to PLANE as CAVER is to: Crave • Caper • Cover • Carve • Caves

GLUTTONY is to SIN as CHARITY is to: Love • Kindness • Virtue • Justice • Generosity

TWENTY is to CHINA as THIRTY is to: Gold • Hong Kong • Ruby • Japan • Pearl

BULGE is to GLUE as PARTY is to: Tory • Tray • Trap • Rave • Ball

106

Memory Jog

Spend two minutes memorising this list of twenty words, then see how many of them you can recall on a separate piece of paper in another two minutes.

FIFTY	FAR	ACCEPT	LAUDABLE
OPEN	DECIMAL	ORIGIN	PLENTIFUL
WILL	REVISION	STOLEN	ENDING
PROBABLE	AUDIBLE	REALLY	ORANGE
TIME	SCREEN	DELAY	VENISON

Shape Up

Can you arrange these five-letter shapes into their correct positions in the grid so that ten **London boroughs** read down the columns?

TIME

WORKOUT 101

Codewords   TIME

If **WATER=12345** and **TONIC=36789**, how quickly can you work out these drinks? You should identify more letters as you go along.

1. 3 4 2
2. 1 8 7 4
3. 9 8 10 4 5
4. 11 6 10 2
5. 5 4 3 11 8 7 2

Scramble   TIME

What geographical terms can be made from each of these sets of scrambled letters?

1. PACE
2. LEAD
3. STEW
4. HORSE
5. RESTED
6. MASTER
7. EPIC COP
8. USE TRAY
9. SWAP CON
10. DRAGSLEEVE

Pyramid   TIME

Each answer except the first uses all the letters – usually in a different order – from the previous answer plus one extra letter.

1. First vowel
2. Thank you
3. Took a seat
4. Cures leather
5. Holy patron – England's is George
6. Infusion of camomile leaves or barley water
7. Baltic republic, capital Tallinn
8. Deferential
9. Male singers

Fitword

TIME

When all of the listed words have been placed correctly in the grid, which one is left over?

3 letters
Ask
Buy
Kin
Koi
Raw
Vow

4 letters
Idea
Yeti

5 letters
Clown
Daily
Dross
Fused
Havoc
Onset

6 letters
Agency
Gargle
Hereby

7 letters
Artwork
~~Basmati~~

8 letters
Biannual
Staffing

Alpha-Beater

TIME

Every letter of the alphabet has been removed from this crossword. How quickly can you put all 26 back? Use the A-Z list to cross off letters as you use them.

WORKOUT 103

Pathfinder

TIME

Beginning with ANEMONE, and moving up, down, left or right, one letter at a time, can you trace a path of eighteen flowers?

D	A	F	F	I	L	S	I	A	M	O
A	I	N	O	D	D	E	E	R	F	N
A	B	O	Y	L	A	Q	U	I	L	T
I	E	G	B	I	H	N	O	E	R	B
X	I	S	L	L	L	S	J	T	I	A
R	O	U	U	A	I	U	C	C	A	L
D	P	L	E	B	L	L	O	R	I	L
W	G	O	I	E	A	I	U	M	C	S
O	L	A	D	L	L	E	N	A	C	E
N	I	L	E	N	E	N	O	M	O	T
S	P	U	T	I	R	A	N	E	N	I

Futoshiki

TIME

Fill the blank squares so that each row and column contains all the numbers 1, 2 and 3. Use the given numbers and the symbols that tell you if the number in the square is larger (>) or smaller (<) than the number next to it.

Small Change

TIME

Can you change one letter of each of these words to make five new words with a common theme?

1   MERRY • MUG • JUNE • CANON • TALKER

2   DUNE • THICK • COW • WHEAT • GULP

3   SHOW • FRONT • HAIR • RUIN • SHEET

4   BRAWN • CRAG • CLAY • TINKLE • CACKLE

Disavowel

TIME

Can you complete this puzzle by adding all the vowels?
There are **12 As, 13 Es, 6 Is, 12 Os and 3 Us** in the puzzle.

	B			■	P	L		R		L
R					■		N		V	
	S	T	R		L	■	D			S
L		R		D		H		R	D	
■	N			D				■		R
		■		■	T	W		N		■
R		C		C		■		G	R	
	S	H	L		R		N			
■		■	D	R			S	T		B
R		N		G				V		
■	R		R		S		R	Y		

Sudoku

TIME

Use your powers of reasoning to place numbers in the grid, so that each row, each column and each 3x3 block contains the numbers 1-9.

								5
8	3		7				1	
		2		9			3	
	8			1	3	9	4	7
4								1
9	7	1	6	4			5	
	4			8		1		
	5				9		2	4
7								

Three in One

TIME

The three parts of each clue lead to the same answer word. Can you solve any before you reach the third part?

1 Draft of a proposed law • Beak • Invoice

2 Professorship • Person in charge of a meeting • Seat

3 Prevalent • Piece of land for public use • Vulgar

4 Tolerate • Erode • Have on as clothing

5 Short period • Charm • Name letters of a word in order

WORKOUT 105

Mini Fit TIME

Which one of the listed words won't fit in each of these mini grids?

OUT
TOW
TWO
TUT
WIT

FLU
FLY
FRY
FUR
RYE

ALLY
LEAD
LILY
LORD
REAL

CHIN
CORN
EACH
HAIR
IRON

Wordsearch TIME

Hidden in this wordsearch grid are fifteen Greek islands.

S	L	C	N	S	P	S	I	O
O	E	E	N	A	X	O	S	C
M	T	P	G	Z	S	N	S	O
A	E	H	S	E	D	O	H	R
S	R	A	A	O	C	K	V	F
E	C	L	P	S	N	Y	E	U
U	T	O	I	A	S	M	Y	F
M	D	N	R	K	R	O	E	Q
S	K	I	A	T	H	O	S	L
W	C	A	H	Z	A	T	S	J
I	N	I	R	O	T	N	A	S

Codewords TIME

If BEACH=12345 and SHORE=65782, how quickly can you work out these beach words? You should identify another letter as you go along.

1 6 2 3

2 4 8 3 1

3 4 7 3 6 9

4 8 2 6 7 8 9

5 1 3 9 5 2 8 6

Mind the Gap

Can you complete the five words in each set by adding the same three-letter word? For example OUR in HLY, VIG, FTH (hourly, vigour, fourth), and so on.

1 MUY PAA DESY HUNG ROUE

2 DET APEL COME SROW ASAGUS

3 CTY STER EMPIC WSIT LYMPIC

4 ANM FAR CLOD WEAR APARID

5 CHAI SULA FOOTH IMIENT COMIBLE

Memory Quiz

TIME

Here's a quiz to see how much attention you're really paying to your surroundings. No peeping!

1 Which creature appears on the Barclays Bank logo?

2 What is depicted on the tails side of the one pence piece?

3 *Eastenders*, *East-enders*, *East-Enders* or *EastEnders*: which is the correct spelling of the BBC soap opera?

4 What colour is a standard 2nd class stamp?

5 Who wore glasses, Morecambe or Wise?

6 Which colour or colours appears after plain amber on a traffic light?

Kakuro

TIME

Simple addition and a bit of logical thinking will solve this one. You must write a digit in each white square so that the digits in each across section add up to the total in the triangle to the left, and the digits in each column add up to the total in the triangle above. 1-9 are the only digits to use and, although you may find a digit repeated in a row, it must not be repeated in the same section. We've solved one section for you.

WORKOUT 107

Arroword

Just follow the arrows to write your answers in the grid. A handful of anagram clues will get you thinking differently.

Angola's continent ▼	World superpower (inits) ▼	CARS (anag) ▼	Keeps happy	▼	Urban horizon	Loud piercing cry
Patties of seafood and potato ▶				▼		▼
__ Maria, coffee liqueur	Partner in war	Singer Ms Winehouse ▶			NEAT (anag)	
▶	▼	Frozen water	Person who reigns ▶		▼	
Short piece (of video) ▶				TIES (anag)		
			Reddish dye used on hair			
▶						
Bathroom powder	Japanese currency ▶			Fabric joint ▶		

Vowel Play

Can you replace the missing vowels to complete these dogs?

1 P G
2 B X R
3 C R G
4 B G L
5 C L L
6 L R C H R
7 S M Y D
8 L S T N
9 R T R V R
10 T R R R

Codewords

If **KILO is 1234** and **ROMEO is 54674**, how quickly can you work out these NATO phonetic alphabet words? You should identify more letters as you go along.

1 6217
2 3268
3 79104
4 1127558
5 91085327

Wordsearch

How quickly can you find the seven themed words in each grid?

DIAMONDS

D	Z	Q	H	D	Y	C
B	L	U	X	Y	N	O
M	G	A	R	N	E	T
I	L	R	R	U	S	A
J	A	T	L	E	B	U
N	P	Z	V	X	M	Y
T	O	P	A	Z	O	E

CLUBS

W	P	J	H	R	T	Y
E	G	U	S	R	T	O
R	A	U	O	E	P	X
C	U	U	I	R	D	E
G	P	C	N	L	G	K
E	O	B	A	N	D	Z
S	E	L	C	R	I	C

SPADES

L	M	N	E	S	F	M
F	E	O	O	R	O	J
X	H	V	W	A	R	Q
V	Z	S	O	E	K	W
E	K	A	R	H	R	G
U	I	B	R	S	S	A
T	R	O	W	E	L	H

Letter Sequence

What letter should replace the question mark in these sequences?

1 B, D, H, K, M, Q, ?

2 A, N, C, P, ?, S, J, W

3 E, R, F, ?, G, W, H

4 R, O, Y, G, B, I, ?

5 G, W, V, E, G, E, G, ?

Four by Four

How quickly can you solve this mini crossword?

1	2	3	4
5			
6			
7			

ACROSS

1 Grow boring
5 Opera song
6 Rain heavily
7 Metal fastener

DOWN

1 Footway
2 Zone, region
3 Falsehoods
4 Bedside light

WORKOUT 109

Pairs

Pair off 24 of the listed words to form twelve "double-barrelled" words and rearrange the letters of the two words left over to reveal **a safety exit**.

BACK	GAMMON	ROYAL
BEAN	MANNERS	RUNNER
BIKE	MARINE	SAFE
BIRTH	MARKET	STONE
BLACK	MAT	STRING
CARD	MOUNTAIN	TABLE
DAY	PENNY	VEST
DOOR	POLE	VISITING
FRONT	RECIPE	

Splits

Can you rearrange each of these sets of letter blocks into a word?

1 DE BAR CA RI

2 EN TE UN CIA

3 US ING EN IO

4 ING AT UR FE

5 OU DE HI SLY

Box Wise

Can you place the three-letter groups in the boxes, so that neighbouring boxes always make a six-letter word, like PAR-DON or DON-ATE? We've placed one group to start you off.

ATE	DON	ING	ROT
BUT	EEM	KEY	TEN
CAR	EST	~~PAR~~	TON

116

Mini Jigsaw

TIME

Fit the pieces in the grid to spell out an item of clothing in each row.

So Complete

TIME

Complete each trio of words with a common letter. The five letters will form the answer word. Where there is a choice of completing letter, you must decide which is needed.

DRA_	DA_N	S_AN	
W_ITE	AS_EN	_OIST	
PA_N	SH_FT	L_KE	
MORA_S	CARE_S	CHA_E	
_ING	WIN_	S_IN	

WORKOUT 111

Word Builder

Using the nine letters provided, can you answer these clues? Every answer must include the highlighted letter M. Which type of creature uses all nine letters?

L	A	R
I	M	P
S	U	A

5 Letters
OT song
Baby buggies
Trade downturn
Light-splitting device
Tia ___, coffee-flavoured liqueur
Posts
Dark purple stone fruits

6 Letters
Wall paintings
Liquid part of blood
Spicy sausage
Fundamental, original
Warning sounds

7 Letters
Medieval Japanese feudal warriors
African antelopes

Take Five

The three answers in this mini-crossword read the same across and down. We've clued the three answers, but not in the right order. See how quickly you can solve it.

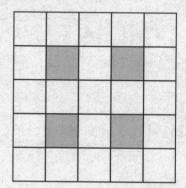

Auctioneer's hammer

Eagle's claw

Number in an octet

Wild Words

`TIME`

What well-known phrases and expressions are suggested by these word pictures?

1 LIfe KiNg   R O A D S

2 111111 other other other other other other

3 ROADS

4 AcCAUGHTt

Missing Link

`TIME`

The three words in each clue have a fourth word in common, and that's your answer. For example, the clue 'Moon • Navy • Royal' gives the answer BLUE (blue moon, navy blue, royal blue). Write each answer in the grid, and the shaded column will reveal a fruit.

1 Comfort • Shoulder • Stone

2 Cap • Deep • Jerk

3 Free • Half • Lag

4 Log • Open • Rest

5 Dock • Mine • Lady

1				
2				
3				
4				
5				

Elimination

`TIME`

All but two of the listed words fall into one of the four categories. Put these leftover words together, and what word or phrase do they make?

CATEGORIES Body part anagrams • Green things • Words following OIL (eg Seed) • Square numbers

Sixteen	Keen	Lime	Viler	Nine	Emerald
Rig	Grass	Step	Earth	Skin	Jade
Two	Olive	Drum	Twenty-five	Well	
Lose	One	Slick	Café	Four	

WORKOUT 113

Mini Fit

Which one of the listed words won't fit in each of these mini grids?

DEN
DUE
END
NOD
ODE

APT
ATE
PAT
SET
SIP

Memory Jog

You have two minutes to study the list of twenty words. Then give yourself another two minutes to write as many as you can recall on a separate piece of paper.

UPSTAIRS	OBVIOUSLY	QUALITY	VERIFY	TOOTH
ANOTHER	OAR	RAIN	OUTSIDE	PUPPY
LAMP	ACORN	BLOOD	MOREOVER	STALL
PICTURE	REMINDER	CLIP	COUNT	LEAF

Cell Blocks

Fill the grid by drawing blocks along the gridlines. Each block must be square or rectangular and must contain the number of squares indicated by the digit inside it. Each block must contain only one digit.

Sudoku

TIME

Place a number in each empty square so that each row, each column and each 2x2 block contains all the numbers from 1-4.

3			2
	4	3	
	3	2	
4			3

4	
4	3
2	4

4			
		2	
		1	
	2		

Add Up

TIME

If the number in each circle is the sum of the two below it, how quickly can you figure out the top number? Try this one in your head, before writing anything down.

TIME ▢

Codeword

Can you crack the code and fill in the crossword grid? Each letter of the alphabet makes at least one appearance in the grid, and is represented by the same number wherever it appears. The four letters we've decoded should help you to identify other letters and words in the grid.

A̶ B C D̶ E F G H I J K L M N O P Q R S̶ T U V W̶ X Y Z

1	2	3	4	5	6 W	7	8	9	10 A	11	12	13
14	15	16	17	18	19	20	21	22 S	23	24 D	25	26

Spot the Sum

TIME ▢

In each of these boxes, one of the numbers is the sum of two others. Can you spot the sum?

1
16 8 3 27 34
23 10 9 14

2
8 11 20 16 13
18 4 6 23

3
19 17 4 12 24
18 9 25 14

4
26 11 1 36 32
5 19 9 13 29

Niners

Form four nine-letter words using all twelve listed "syllables" (without altering the order of the letters in each "syllable"). Then enter them in the grid in the right order to reveal **the sound of a donkey** reading down the **left-hand** column.

AIL   AUT   BLA

CKM   DAY   ISH

LEN   OMA   REP

TER   TON   YES

Mane Line

Which numbered photograph has been taken?

WORKOUT 117

Mobile Code

If HARRISON is 42774766 on this phone keypad, which famous Georges have the following numbers?

1 2653

2 2566639

3 367629

4 3673626

5 6424235

6 7377273

Logical

How quickly can you figure out what's what?

There are three particularly popular pigs at a local country farm. From the information given below, work out how long each pig has been at the farm (three, four or five years), their favourite activity and which pigpen they sleep in.

Trotter has been at the farm longer than Hambo, whose favourite activity is truffle hunting. The mudbath isn't the activity of choice for Curly, the pig that has spent five years at the farm. The pig that stays in the West pen enjoys football, while the pig in the North pen has spent a year longer at the farm than the pig in the South pen.

Honeycomb

Write the six-letter answers clockwise round their respective cell-numbers, starting at the arrowed cell. On completion, you will find that the unclued answers (10 and 11) will reveal **someone of lesser importance – in the strings?**

1 Three times over
2 Tame and placid
3 Tended the sick
4 Nearly
5 Delphi's prophetic shrine
6 Sheep's shorn coat
7 Bestow
8 Game bird
9 Dried grape

Fitword

TIME

When all of the listed words have been placed correctly in the grid, which one is left over?

3 letters
Dew
Ill
Inn

4 letters
Bred
Edgy
Know
Load

Luge
Maim
~~Rump~~
Tsar
Used
Yoga

7 letters
Firmest
Magical

Slowing
Steered

9 letters
Ascending
Silliness

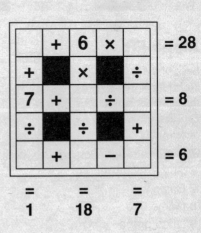

Set Square

TIME

Place one each of the digits 1-9 in the grid to make the sums work. We've put in some of the numbers to start you off. Sums should be solved from left to right, or from top to bottom.

	+	6	×		= 28
+		×		÷	
7	+		÷		= 8
÷		÷		+	
	+		−		= 6

= 1   = 18   = 7

WORKOUT 119

Pathfinder

TIME

Beginning with MAORI, and moving up, down, left or right, one letter at a time, can you trace a path of nineteen languages?

D	E	W	S	M	A	Y	N	A	R	E
I	R	U	I	R	O	S	W	M	O	S
S	K	T	I	L	I	H	A	A	N	E
H	I	S	L	A	N	S	H	P	H	C
H	I	H	E	I	D	I	J	A	U	E
D	N	I	C	C	A	N	U	D	R	Z
I	F	L	O	P	P	S	I	A	N	C
E	R	I	H	P	U	I	S	R	H	S
N	C	S	C	T	N	B	S	U	L	I
K	H	H	D	U	J	A	E	L	G	N
A	S	H	M	I	R	I	W	S	H	E

Number Jig

TIME

Which one of the listed numbers won't fit in each of these mini grids?

208		153		1627
284		397		2126
420		531		2272
824		751		6621
842		915		7261

Alpha-Fit

TIME

Each of the 26 letters of the alphabet appears once in this crossword.

ACROSS
2 Cry of a duck (5)
6 Female fox (5)
7 Norwegian inlets (6)

DOWN
1 Adhesive substance (3)
3 French fries (5)
4 Spider's snare (3)
5 Monetary unit of Poland (5)

A	B	C	D	E	F	G	H	I	J	K	L	M
N	O	P	Q	R	S	T	U	V	W	X	Y	Z

126

Pyramid

Each answer except the first uses all the letters – usually in a different order – from the previous answer plus one extra letter.

TIME

1 Food additives number
2 Concerning
3 Keen resentment
4 Old Ireland
5 Coal-face worker
6 Stay
7 Mosque's tower
8 Airport check-in and departure building
9 Outer markings around a tennis court

Sudoku

TIME

Use your powers of reasoning to place numbers in the grid, so that each row, each column and each 3x3 block contains the numbers 1-9.

	7				9			
	2			9	1	7		
1							8	5
		4		2				1
8		6		5		2		4
3			1		6			
7	9							6
		1	6	3			9	
		3			4			

Staircase

TIME

When the seven **rivers** are correctly placed along the horizontal rows, the letters in the diagonal "staircase" will yield an eighth.

DANUBE

DARLING

GANGES

GARONNE

TRENT

YELLOW

ZAMBEZI

WORKOUT 121

Sudoku TIME

Place a number in each empty square so that each row, each column and each 2x2 block contains all the numbers from 1-4.

			3
			1
3			
2			4

Wordsearch TIME

Hidden in this wordsearch grid are fourteen musical instruments.

C	L	A	R	I	N	E	T	I
O	B	O	E	E	D	G	C	R
B	N	Y	K	N	R	L	U	B
E	A	A	D	O	U	O	A	R
T	C	N	I	H	M	S	T	E
U	A	E	J	P	S	M	R	H
L	N	I	L	O	I	V	U	T
F	Z	N	O	L	W	E	M	I
S	J	N	V	Y	O	P	P	Z
P	R	A	H	X	B	X	E	H
G	U	I	T	A	R	F	T	T

Four by Four TIME

How quickly can you solve this mini crossword?

1	2	3	4
5			
6			
7			

ACROSS
1 Electric cable
5 Biblical garden
6 Soft heavy metal
7 ___ Army, classic TV sitcom

DOWN
1 Join (metal) using heat
2 Concept
3 Peruse
4 Terminates

Smart Sums

Try to avoid writing down anything but the final answers to
these calculations… no counting on fingers allowed either!

1 Lines in a sonnet ÷ days in a week

2 Sides on a hexagon + consonants in MEANDER

3 Sections of an orchestra X syllables in ANEMONE

4 Months in 17 years − wheels on a tandem

5 Number of blackbirds baked in a pie X legs on the Manx flag

Opposites Attract

Can you sort each set of letter blocks into two words with opposite meanings?

1 AD BRO ED KE LO

2 TH RA SE ER TO TE PA GE

3 IV IC PU PR ATE BL

4 OP IM RE PR COR ER CT

Kakuro

Simple addition and a bit of logical thinking will solve this one. You must write
a digit in each white square so that the digits in each across section add up to
the total in the triangle to the left, and the digits in each column add up to the
total in the triangle above. 1-9 are the only digits to use and, although you may
find a digit repeated in a row, it must not be repeated in the same section.
We've solved one section for you.

WORKOUT 123

Arroword

Just follow the arrows to write your answers in the grid. A handful of anagram clues will get you thinking differently.

Cut in two ▼	Make a choice ▼	Part of a guitar's fingerboard ▼	Cavort, gambol ▼	Meal period	LATENT (anag)
Flawed ►			▼		▼
Affirmative reply	Pig food	Division of geological time ►		NOVA (anag)	
►		Right, fitting	Final amount ▼		▼
Scallop ►		▼	Reside ►		
		___ Pegg, *Hot Fuzz* star ►			
POTS (anag)	Go to next page (inits) ►		US monetary unit ►		

Splits

Can you rearrange each of these sets of letter blocks into a word?

1. IS ES TS SAY
2. OF RE FI PRO
3. SC AR HOL LY
4. UND RO NA RU
5. RI DEX TY TE

Logical

Try solving this little logical problem in your head before putting pen to paper.

Three friends each won a medal at their school's sports day. If Chuck got silver, but not in the discus, and Sanjeev's long jump got him a higher placing than the contestant in the 100m, which event did Russell take part in, and where did he come?

Cake Bake ⏱TIME

Which two pictures are identical?

1

2

3

4

5

6

Two of a Kind ⏱TIME

Can you sort each set of letter blocks into two words with the same meaning?

1 SO LE MP TE LU AB TE CO

2 CO MAG TE NA ON TY

3 MI NE ST EN TY SS OR VA

4 PER CO NT TA NE MA NS NT

5 OR CH ON VI PI CT AM

Staircase ⏱TIME

When these **furniture items** are correctly fitted in the rows of the grid, another such item will appear down the diagonal staircase.

BENCH

CRADLE

DIVAN

ROCKER

TABLE

TALLBOY

WHATNOT

WORKOUT 125

Fare's Fair

Find two words of the same sound but different spelling to satisfy each two-element clue, then decide which of the pair goes where in the grid to discover **a spice**, reading down the arrowed column.

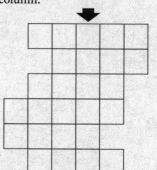

Rule in wet weather

Equitable cost of a journey

Occasion for a herb

Lazy false god

Of sound mind at the river

Correct ceremonial procedure

Memory Jog

Give yourself two minutes to memorise this list of thirty words. How many of them can you recall on a separate piece of paper in another two minutes?

BELLOW	ALTOGETHER
WHITHER	APPLE
FROND	BRACKET
GUIDE	FLASHY
HATSTAND	STEERING
DILIGENTLY	PERSEVERANCE
ROCK	DESPOND
SCREEN	PENCIL
DISCO	FASHION
TYPE	GREETING
CLATTER	PERSIST
STEW	SLANG
QUESTIONNAIRE	RAFFLE
PLAYHOUSE	CREEPY
WOBBLY	
SINCE	

Futoshiki

Fill the blank squares so that each row and column contains all the numbers 1, 2 and 3. Use the given numbers and the symbols that tell you if the number in the square is larger (>) or smaller (<) than the number next to it.

Mini Jigsaw

TIME

Fit the pieces in the grid to spell out a dessert in each row.

E	T
S	E

T	R
Y	O

S	U
G	A

L	E
R	T

N	D
T	E

R	B
U	S

I	F
G	U

S	O
M	O

A	E
A	U

Grid:
- Row 1 / 2: ... ... E
- Row 3 / 4: ... ... E
- Row 5 / 6: ... E ...

Killer Sudoku

TIME

The normal rules of Sudoku apply. Place a digit from 1-9 in each empty square so that each row, column and 3x3 block contains all the digits from 1-9. In addition, the digits in each inner shape (marked by dots) must add up to the number in the top corner of that box. No digit can be repeated within an inner shape.

WORKOUT 127

Word Builder TIME

Using the nine letters provided, can you answer these clues? Every answer must include the highlighted letter C. Which form of betterment uses all nine letters?

I	D	E
A	C	U
N	O	T

5 Letters
Caper
Move to music
Sharp
Make into law
Vast sea
Gin accompaniment
Small narrow boat

6 Letters
Big-billed bird
Director's cry
Church official
Persuade, talk into
Petrol ingredient

7 Letters
Espied
Added up
Tube for carrying fluid

9 Letters
Warned
Sold to the highest bidder

Wordsearch TIME

How quickly can you find the seven themed words in each grid?

ROYAL

I	S	N	G	R	P	S
D	I	T	C	N	R	M
Q	U	E	E	N	I	O
J	Q	K	O	K	N	K
V	R	R	E	Q	C	F
Y	A	L	R	A	E	H
B	M	B	U	D	P	X

OPERA

O	L	L	E	T	O	H
N	N	C	X	T	T	T
O	E	Z	D	E	O	F
R	M	U	B	S	A	A
M	R	C	C	K	D	U
A	A	A	G	M	I	S
M	C	I	J	H	A	T

HOUSE

C	O	O	L	G	I	I
N	O	I	S	N	A	M
T	M	T	L	S	H	E
Y	A	W	T	C	N	S
V	I	L	L	A	X	A
O	E	J	F	D	G	K
B	E	D	S	I	T	E

Niners

Form four nine-letter words using all twelve listed "syllables" (without altering the order of the letters in each "syllable"). Then enter them in the grid in the right order to reveal **a European capital city** reading down the **left-hand** column.

AGE	CEM	EAS
EAT	ECT	HAN
MIN	OLL	ORP
RDS	REC	TWA

Set Square

Place one each of the digits 1-9 in the grid to make the sums work. We've put in some of the numbers to start you off. Sums should be solved from left to right, or from top to bottom.

	×		÷		= 14
+		−		+	
	+		−	5	= 5
−		×		÷	
6	×		−		= 9

= 10   = 14   = 3

Elimination

All but two of the listed words fall into one of the four categories. Put these leftover words together, and what phrase do they make?

CATEGORIES Santa's reindeer • Words preceding BALL (eg foot) • Egg-laying creatures • Dances

Hand	Boy	Bee	Dasher	Tango	Samba
Goose	Vixen	Screw	Odd	Dancer	Punch
Foxtrot	Pin	Jive	Cupid	Principal	
Comet	Waltz	Turtle	Platypus	Salmon	

135

WORKOUT 129

Wordsearch

How quickly can you find the five themed words in each grid?

BIG ___

U	M	B	A	N	G	B
X	D	O	N	T	R	Z
Y	I	Q	U	O	T	G
K	P	W	T	T	O	P
J	P	H	L	S	H	B
R	E	F	M	E	S	C
R	R	I	V	D	O	H

SMALL ___

E	R	A	T	X	J	F
G	H	E	C	I	O	Z
N	R	E	E	R	M	V
A	O	W	T	B	I	E
H	L	U	F	R	Y	Q
C	N	K	Y	S	T	B
E	M	P	D	F	N	U

Pairs

TIME

Pair off 24 of the listed words to form twelve "double-barrelled" words and rearrange the letters of the two words left over to reveal **a condiment**.

ARM	FIELD	SCARLET	CENTRE	LINE	WINDOW	EAGLE
FEVER	REST	BREAK	GERM	VALIANT	DOWN	OUT
PITCH	BOW	GARDEN	TIE	CRICKET	NECK	
BORDER	FRENCH	SPREAD	CHAIR	MARKET	WOMAN	

Cell Blocks

TIME

Fill the grid by drawing blocks along the gridlines. Each block must be square or rectangular and must contain the number of squares indicated by the digit inside it. Each block must contain only one digit.

Sudoku TIME

Place a number in each empty square so that each row, each column and each 2x2 block contains all the numbers from 1-4.

1			2
	2	4	
	1	2	
2			4

4			2
	2	1	
	4	2	
2			1

4			3
	3	4	
	1	3	
3			1

Add Up TIME

If the number in each circle is the sum of the two below it, how quickly can you figure out the top number? Try this one in your head, before writing anything down.

WORKOUT 131

Codeword

Can you crack the code and fill in the crossword grid? Each letter of the alphabet makes at least one appearance in the grid, and is represented by the same number wherever it appears. The four letters we've decoded should help you to identify other letters and words in the grid.

A̶ B C̶ D E F G H I J K L M N̶ O P Q R̶ S T U V W X Y Z

1	2 C	3	4	5	6 R	7	8	9	10	11	12	13
14	15 N	16	17	18	19	20	21	22	23	24	25 A	26

Grid clue letters shown: R A N C

Memory Quiz

Here's a quiz to see how much attention you're really paying to your surroundings. No peeping!

1 In Coronation Street, what colour is the exterior of the Rovers Return Inn painted?

2 On the Welsh flag, does the dragon face left or right?

3 Which is the correct spelling – brocolli, broccolli, broccoli or brocoli?

4 Does Prime Minister Gordon Brown part his hair on the left or the right?

5 Which denomination bank note contains portraits of two women?

6 In general, what colour is the lid on a plastic bottle of skimmed milk?

TIME

Splits

TIME

Can you rearrange each of these sets of letter blocks into a word?

1 HE PER RY IP   4 NAG ME IE ER
2 RE CH CA ILD   5 RED AT WE HE
3 NEE TI MU RS

Baby Face

TIME

Which numbered photograph has been taken?

WORKOUT 133

Number Sequence TIME

What number should replace the question mark in these sequences?

1 1, 5, 14, 30, 55, ?

2 1, 9, 7, 16, 13, 23, 19, ?

3 7, 8, 5, 5, 3, 4, 4, ?

4 ...6, 4, 8, 14, 18, 26, 40, ?

5 ...10, 14, 22, 38, ?, 134

Initials TIME

If ITHOTN (Oscar-winning film) is *IN THE HEAT OF THE NIGHT*, what do these initials represent?

1 KK (Film monster)

2 OAL (Nursery school song)

3 TLD (Scenic area)

4 TLTOP (World landmark)

5 JATATD (Musical)

Pyramid TIME

Each answer except the first uses all the letters – usually in a different order – from the previous answer plus one extra letter.

1 Spain's vehicle registration letter

2 Musical note

3 Game, ___ and match

4 Remainder

5 Guide

6 Difficult question

7 (Of leaves) having a sawlike edge

8 Move across a mountain face

9 Reaper

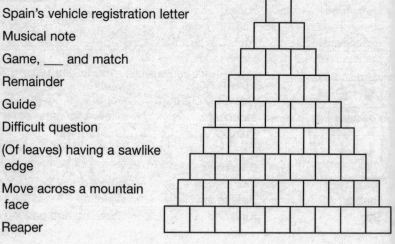

Fitword

TIME

When all of the listed words have been placed correctly in the grid, which one is left over?

3 letters

Bad

But

Ebb

Its

Sob

Tea

4 letters

Also

Rode

Room

Snob

Stay

Yips

5 letters

Basil

Catty

Cocoa

Farce

Gusto

Mogul

~~Rogue~~

Sides

Tasty

7 letters

Cramped

Tinting

Word Builder

TIME

Using the nine letters provided, can you answer these clues? Every answer must include the highlighted letter N. Which law enforcer uses all nine letters?

V	E	G
A	N	I
L	I	T

Ask to come

Knot (of hair, eg)

Involve

Belly-button

Heavenly creature

Innocent

Point of view

5 Letters

Foreign

Spy

6 Letters

Indigenous

Set fire to

Kind

7 Letters

Departing

Classic (of cars, eg)

Shadowing

Masking

8 Letters

Watchful

Cleaning and parking cars

WORKOUT 135

Pathfinder

TIME

Beginning with FARFALLE, and moving up, down, left or right, one letter at a time, can you trace a path of fifteen types of pasta?

L	I	E	N	G	A	S	R	A	M	I
L	R	R	R	E	R	A	O	C	A	L
E	A	A	O	G	I	L	N	I	I	L
M	V	D	T	A	E	S	O	N	S	U
E	I	I	A	T	L	D	O	A	L	F
G	O	L	I	O	F	A	R	F	L	E
I	L	H	G	N	L	I	E	L	H	I
E	L	E	A	I	G	A	T	L	C	G
C	I	T	P	T	A	I	U	E	N	L
R	M	T	S	S	A	N	G	C	O	I
E	V	I	A	T	P	E	N	I	L	E

Number Jig

TIME

Which one of the listed numbers won't fit in each of these mini grids?

121		293		3689	
125		324		3739	
250		439		6793	
510		492		6837	
515		942		9638	

Leaf Alone

TIME

Can you spot the nine differences between these pictures?

142

Spot the Sum

TIME

In each of these boxes, one of the numbers is the sum of two others. Can you spot the sum?

1

| 7 | 32 | 20 | 1 | 9 |
| | 4 | 15 | 34 | 22 |

3

| 24 | 12 | 4 | 37 | 18 |
| | 30 | 9 | 29 | 23 |

2

| 33 | 18 | 5 | 12 | 29 |
| | 37 | 11 | 3 | 31 |

4

| 6 | 19 | 39 | 15 | 29 |
| | 8 | 35 | 26 | 30 |

Sudoku

TIME

Use your powers of reasoning to place numbers in the grid, so that each row, each column and each 3x3 block contains the numbers 1-9.

4			3	5				2
	2		4	9		8		
5		1				3		7
		8	2		3	9		
	5		7		2		1	
8	1	7				2	9	6
		3		9		5		

Scramble

TIME

The names of which star constellations can be made from each of these sets of scrambled letters? Some will be much more familiar than others!

1 OLE

2 ARISE

3 IN ROO

4 OH GULP

5 SPICES

6 EAGER BRAT (5,4)

7 DEAD ROMAN

8 CAIRN CROP

143

Six Pack `TIME`

Can you place digits in the empty triangles, so that the numbers in each hexagon add up to 25? Only single digits between 1 and 9 can be used, and no two numbers in any hexagon may be the same.

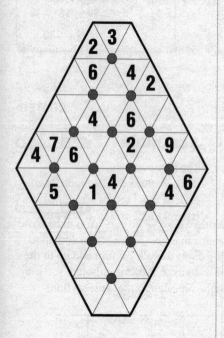

Wordsearch `TIME`

Hidden in this wordsearch grid are fifteen American States.

H	A	W	A	I	I	O	G	M
F	A	F	L	O	R	I	D	A
X	I	R	W	U	A	H	M	V
O	L	A	I	K	R	O	A	E
D	H	D	S	Z	N	J	I	R
A	N	A	T	N	O	M	N	M
E	L	V	D	T	G	N	E	O
A	B	E	T	I	E	O	A	N
N	Q	N	S	W	R	X	C	T
U	T	A	H	K	O	Z	A	A
K	R	O	Y	W	E	N	P	S

Smart Sums `TIME`

Try to avoid writing down anything but the final answers to these calculations…

1 One gross – ounces in 7lbs

2 Days in a leap year – hours in 9 days

3 Suits in a pack of cards x maximum number of spots on a domino

4 Consonants in MAGNANIMOUS + total number of dots on a die

5 Gallons made up by 72 pints x reputed number of lives a cat has

Copycats

Choose the answer that best copies the pattern.

WRITE is to PEN as PLAY is to: Sty • Clarinet • Stage • Theatre • Fool

DOVE is to COTE as HARE is to: Gape • Have • Farm • Lair • Holt

WEMBLEY is to FOOTBALL as LORD'S is to: Tennis • Rugby • Cricket • Golf • Polo

PUMA is to AMERICA as TIGER is to: Europe • France • Asia • Korea • Africa

WATER is to LIQUID as OXYGEN is to: Vapour • Steam • Gas • Breath • Air

Memory Jog

Spend two minutes memorising this list of twenty words, then see how many of them you can recall on a separate piece of paper.

TWIN	OPEN	BRIGHTNESS	TYRE	RANK
PEARL	THINK	HANDLE	OWL	CRATER
GONG	LOUDLY	RADIO	CHAIN	
CREAKING	MOVEMENT	TICKER		
SPEND	FUME	RACKETEER		

Kakuro

Simple addition and a bit of logical thinking will solve this one. You must write a digit in each white square so that the digits in each across section add up to the total in the triangle to the left, and the digits in each column add up to the total in the triangle above. 1-9 are the only digits to use and, although you may find a digit repeated in a row, it must not be repeated in the same section. We've solved one section for you.

WORKOUT 139

Arroword

Just follow the arrows to write your answers in the grid. A handful of anagram clues will get you thinking differently.

Religious writings	Heron-like bird	Bed dress	▼	Commercial channel (inits) ▼		Pop-band follower	▼	SKA (anag)	▼
▶	▼								
Public washing place		Slang word for 'clothing'		Put in the mail		List of actors		Confide in	
▶		▼		▼	Slice or trim	▼		▼	Rob ___, Scottish hero
Jotting sheets									▼
▶					SOIL (anag) ▶				
BINGE (anag)	In a calm controlled way ▶								

Vowel Play

Can you replace the missing vowels to complete the names of these herbs and spices?

1 B Y
2 M C
3 M N T
4 S G
5 N S

6 B R G
7 N S D
8 R G N
9 R S M R Y
10 T R M R C

Small Change

Can you change one letter of each of these words to make five new words with a common theme?

1 HALF • LEFT • CLAMBER • QUITE • COLLAR
2 BLOOD • STALE • METAL • LOAF • SEND
3 SORE • TONE • LOGGER • DOWER • BAILED
4 HEATING • COUCH • RIGHT • WASTE • SMALL
5 JOB • BLESS • GLUE • CAPTURE • EXALTATION

146

Fix Six TIME

The six **animals** listed will fit into this pattern of six adjoining hexagons. All are entered clockwise from a triangle to be discovered. Adjoining triangles always contain the same letter. The **K** gives you a start.

BADGER   GERBIL

COUGAR   OCELOT

FERRET   SALUKI

Mobile Code TIME

If ODD is 633 on this phone keypad, what mathematical terms have the following numbers?

1 786

2 6326

3 7668

4 82583

5 628749

Four by Four TIME

How quickly can you solve this mini crossword?

1	2	3	4
5			
6			
7			

ACROSS

1 Reserve
5 Peak, apex
6 Curds and ___, Miss Muffet's lunch
7 Part of the eye

DOWN

1 Yell
2 Darts players' line
3 Forewarning
4 Typewriter levers

Set Square [TIME]

Place one each of the digits 1-9 in the grid to make the sums work. We've put in some of the numbers to start you off. Sums should be solved from left to right, or from top to bottom.

	−		×		= 36
−	■	×	■	÷	
1	×		÷		= 2
×	■	÷	■	+	
	×	2	−		= 3

= 35   = 12   = 10

Take Five [TIME]

The three answers in this mini-crossword read the same across and down. We've clued the three answers, but not in the right order. See how quickly you can solve it.

Well done!

Black wood

Item of furniture

Mind the Gap [TIME]

Can you place a well-known three-letter word in the spaces of each row to complete the seven-letter word? Do it correctly, and the shaded letters should spell out something associated with Advent.

S	E				E	D
D	E				N	T
D	E	P				E
T	R	O				R
S				G	L	E
M	A				N	S
H	O				R	S
R	E				O	F

Mini Jigsaw

Fit the pieces in the grid to spell out something found in the kitchen in each row.

Killer Sudoku

The normal rules of Sudoku apply. Place a digit from 1-9 in each empty square so that each row, column and 3x3 block contains all the digits from 1-9. In addition, the digits in each inner shape (marked by dots) must add up to the number in the top corner of that box. No digit can be repeated within an inner shape.

Mini Fit

Which one of the listed words won't fit in each of these mini grids?

AWN
FUN
IDE
USE
WIN

APT
CAP
COW
LAP
OWL

BEST
CART
CUBE
RUSH
WASH

APSE
GLUE
KNEE
OPAL
SPIN

Dominoes

Solve the clues then write the six-letter answers into the dominoes. You must work out whether each word fits in clockwise or anticlockwise, so that the connecting letters of the dominoes all match up.

1 Spanish rice dish with shellfish, chicken and vegetables

2 Chinese edible fruit with a whitish juicy pulp

3 Kidney-shaped nut

4 A blackcurrant cordial

5 Dried grape

6 Italian grilled sandwich

Step Riddle

Can you solve the riddle in five easy steps?

To begin with, I am green fruits, and am found upon a tree. __ __ __ __ __

When you change my first I develop into a daily. __ __ __ __ __

Change a second and you'll find you can still read lots of me. __ __ __ __ __

Alter my third and sound qualities appear. __ __ __ __ __

Swap a fourth letter and I'm useful for curling hair. __ __ __ __ __

At the last, change my last and an island you'll see. __ __ __ __ __

What was I, what did I change into and what did I turn out to be?

Box Wise

Can you place the three-letter groups in the boxes, so that neighbouring boxes always make a six-letter word, like PAR-DON or DON-ATE? We've placed one group to start you off.

DEN	GAR	MAL	STO
DER	ICE	RAP	TAL
ENT	LET	RED	WAR

Soundalikes

Can you complete each of these sentences with two words that sound alike, but are spelled differently?

1 The ____ around Elizabeth I's neck was too ____ for the royal skin.

2 The ____ takeaway we have is Chinese, particularly chow ____.

3 Old Mother Hubbard ____ a large pot of tea for her ever-increasing ____ of children.

4 There's no need to ____ about the quality of ____ if it's from a French vineyard.

WORKOUT 145

Wordsearch

How quickly can you find the five themed words in each grid?

BREAD

B	H	L	E	G	A	B
F	L	B	L	T	L	N
A	C	O	T	O	A	S
O	Q	I	O	K	R	R
L	P	W	U	M	F	P
X	J	G	Z	M	E	O
I	E	D	V	Y	T	R

BUTTER

C	R	E	A	M	Y	O
Y	H	Q	K	O	R	X
E	C	E	G	L	F	T
H	D	U	E	H	I	Z
W	R	K	N	S	M	M
T	W	P	G	V	E	I
J	A	Y	U	B	E	L

Splits

Can you rearrange each of these sets of letter blocks into a word?

1 ER PRE NT SE   **4** RAP HY GE OG

2 IN CE POR LA   **5** NI STO MA FE

3 DER RI AN CO

Cell Blocks

Fill the grid by drawing blocks along the gridlines. Each block must be square or rectangular and must contain the number of squares indicated by the digit inside it. Each block must contain only one digit.

Sudoku   TIME

Place a number in each empty
square so that each row, each
column and each 2x2 block
contains all the numbers from 1-4.

4	3	1	2
2	4	3	1

4			1
	1	4	
	2	1	
1			2

	4	1	
1			3
4			1
	1	3	

Add Up   TIME

If the number in each circle is
the sum of the two below it, how
quickly can you figure out the top
number? Try this one in your head,
before writing anything down.

3		2		22		13		16		4		2
6 G	13	9	1	13	9	9	19	1		19	21	19
9 N		3		24		23		19		5		14
18 O	23	10	3	24	11	20		19	8	13	25	19
1 R			3		13			19			25	
19	20	16		9	3	6	15	10	24	11	23	
	20		24				19		10			
	16	18	18	10	21	19	11	1		15	18	25
11		13			9		1		3			
4	11	9	12	18		6	20	11	17	3	9	6
18		24		11		11		23		10		19
26	3	19		22	18	6	6	3	9	19	22	22
19		25		10		19		9		7		10

A B C D E F Ø H I J K L M Ø Ø P Ø S T U V W X Y Z

1 R	2	3	4	5	6 G	7	8	9 N	10	11	12	13
14	15	16	17	18 O	19	20	21	22	23	24	25	26

TIME

Codeword

Can you crack the code and fill in the crossword grid? Each letter of the alphabet makes at least one appearance in the grid, and is represented by the same number wherever it appears. The four letters we've decoded should help you to identify other letters and words in the grid.

Three in One

TIME

The three parts of each clue lead to the same answer word. Can you solve any before you reach the third part?

1. Instance • Lawsuit • Protective container
2. Enclosure • Write • Female swan
3. Shoemaker's item • Endure • Final
4. Hard stone • Gas or liquid from a nozzle • Aeroplane
5. Detain • Wrestling move • Ship's cargo store

Memory Jog

Spend two minutes memorising this list of twenty words, then see how many of them you can recall on a separate piece of paper in another two minutes.

AFTERNOON	TOMFOOLERY	CHORTLE	BUTTERFLY
PHYSICS	STATUE	CRACKER	DRAMATIC
OCTOBER	REALISING	WALLPAPER	CAUTION
RAIN	GRAVEL	SILENTLY	EXHAUSTIVE
TEA	SPLATTER	CASCADE	TRAINER

Shape Up

Can you arrange these five-letter shapes into their correct positions in the grid so that **five hats and five shoes** read down the columns?

TIME

155

WORKOUT 149

Futoshiki TIME

Fill the blank squares so that each row and column contains all the numbers 1, 2, 3 and 4. Use the given numbers and the symbols that tell you if the number in the square is larger (>) or smaller (<) than the number next to it.

Codewords TIME

If **RICE=1234** and **SNAP=5678**, how quickly can you work out these food words? You should identify one more letter as you go along.

1 8 4 7

2 3 9 1 6

3 3 7 8 4 1

4 3 1 2 5 8

5 5 3 9 6 4

Town to Town TIME

Can you travel from **Dalston** to **West Ham** by removing or adding one letter at each stage from the definitions below, which are consequent anagrams?

D	A	L	S	T	O	N

1 Claws of birds of prey　**1**

2 Singing voices　**2**

3 Final　**3**

4 Posed　**4**

5 Afternoon meals　**5**

6 Detests　**6**

7 London's river　**7**

W	E	S	T	H	A	M

156

Fitword

When all of the listed words have been placed correctly in the grid, which one is left over?

3 letters
Gig
Tut

4 letters
Asti
Body
Fray
Garb
Idly

Iota
Lobe
Lurk

5 letters
~~Ashen~~
Expat
Noted
Rosti

7 letters
Emperor
Tearing
Tipping

9 letters
Beseeched
Sarcastic
Superstar

Spot the Sum

In each of these boxes, one of the numbers is the sum of two others. Can you spot the sum?

1

27 33 20 9 19
14 16 15 12

3

38 18 5 11 3
25 12 31 21

2

10 1 27 7 33
12 21 18 4

4

5 6 28 9 24
13 20 31 34

WORKOUT 151

Pathfinder

Beginning with SUSPECT, and moving up, down, left or right, one letter at a time, can you trace a path of seventeen Cluedo words?

D	G	N	I	P	D	A	E	L	R	E
I	N	I	P	N	I	T	D	A	G	G
N	I	O	M	N	U	O	R	M	U	L
G	R	O	W	O	D	P	E	S	S	P
O	P	A	E	H	W	E	F	O	O	R
N	U	D	D	R	O	M	P	R	T	R
S	T	Y	C	A	O	R	U	S	C	E
N	E	R	H	A	L	L	S	P	E	V
N	A	O	V	L	A	B	I	L	R	E
S	P	L	E	L	B	R	E	N	E	N
R	E	V	R	Y	R	A	E	R	G	D

Add Up

If the number in each circle is the sum of the two below it, how quickly can you figure out the top number? Try this one in your head, before writing anything down.

In and Out

Without changing the order of the letters, add or remove one letter each time to leave a (different) new complete word and put the added or removed letters in their respective boxes to find **a sales outlet** reading down the boxes.

DANE		ROUSE	
NICHE		PLEA	
GLEN		SHOUT	
CLAM		SPIES	
VINE		WEAVE	

158

Complete Works

Complete each trio of words with a common letter. The five letters will form the answer word. Where there is a choice of completing letter, you must decide which is needed.

RIC_	S_AM	BAS_	
SHE_R	L_VER	_MBER	
DRI_E	ALI_E	A_ERT	
STR_P	ST_UT	CH_IR	
PRI_E	_LICK	_HEAT	

Sudoku

Use your powers of reasoning to place numbers in the grid, so that each row, each column and each 3x3 block contains the numbers 1-9.

				5	4			
		9	6				2	1
		2		1		6		
9	3	1		8		7	6	
4	2	5		7		8	3	
		3		9		5		
		8	4				1	7
				6	7			

Four by Four

How quickly can you solve this mini crossword?

1	2	3	4
5			
6			
7			

ACROSS
1 Farm animals
5 Aid illegally
6 Marine flatfish
7 Be of assistance

DOWN
1 Spending money
2 Twin-reeded woodwind instrument
3 Water source
4 Pace

WORKOUT 153

Word Builder TIME

Using the nine letters provided, can you answer these clues? Every answer must include the highlighted letter F. Which enthralling word uses all nine letters?

5 Letters
Banquet
Exploits, deeds
Small restaurants
Sham attack
Truths
Swoon

6 Letters
Spanish carnival
Do up
Best
Betrothed man
Overrun (with vermin)
Sides of a gem

8 Letters
Most la-di-dah
Avid supporters

Wordsearch TIME

Hidden in this wordsearch grid are fifteen Indian dishes.

A	K	A	S	N	A	H	D	V
D	I	O	B	A	L	T	I	A
N	J	H	R	Z	B	N	M	K
A	C	A	T	M	D	R	A	K
S	N	F	L	A	A	V	D	I
A	D	U	L	F	P	H	R	T
P	Q	O	H	C	R	L	A	W
I	O	A	U	B	A	E	S	L
B	I	R	Y	A	N	I	Z	X
U	R	J	H	E	C	I	R	I
Y	M	P	K	E	E	M	A	N

Splits TIME

Can you rearrange each of these sets of letter blocks into a word?

1 MAN DE NG DI

2 ES ING FR IN

3 GE VE DI STI

4 TA CRE RY SE

5 NE PLE IM CR

160

Sudoku

TIME

Place a number in each empty square so that each row, each column and each 2x2 block contains all the numbers from 1-4.

	3	4	
4			3
1			4
	4	1	

3			1
	1	2	
	3	1	
1			2

2			4
		3	2
		2	4
3			2

Wild Words

What well-known phrases and expressions are suggested by these word pictures?

❶ **EDGE**

❷ **STAND**
I

❸ **ENOB**

❹ **D A M P**

❺

Kakuro

Simple addition and a bit of logical thinking will solve this one. You must write a digit in each white square so that the digits in each across section add up to the total in the triangle to the left, and the digits in each column add up to the total in the triangle above. 1-9 are the only digits to use and, although you may find a digit repeated in a row, it must not be repeated in the same section. We've solved one section for you.

		8	4		15	16		22	13
	4			16			16		
	4		7			16			
45									
6	1	5	4			14			

Arroword

TIME

Just follow the arrows to write your answers in the grid. A handful of anagram clues will get you thinking differently.

Old superpower (inits) ▼		Koala's habitat (3,4) ▼		Person of Hebrew origin ▼		Beirut's country ▼		Poisonous snake ▼	
Cleverness, shrewdness ►		Did an impression of		HEAR (anag)		Deep mud		_ Sampras, tennis great	
			▼		▼	AMP (anag) ►			▼
								Low in spirits	
Fury	Nutty chocolates ►								▼
►					Duty system ►				
Support vocally	Intensified ►								

Initials

TIME

If **ITHOTN** (Oscar-winning film) is *IN THE HEAT OF THE NIGHT*, what do these initials represent?

1 ACGAS (Novel and TV series)

2 PO (Crisp flavour)

3 SHADW (Fictional detective pair)

4 MHWGO (No.1 hit and film theme)

5 AWTEW (Proverb and play)

Vowel Play

TIME

Can you replace the missing vowels to complete these Christmas words?

1 N L   6 G R T T

2 C R L   7 L F

3 R N D R   8 S N T

4 B B L   9 W R T H

5 T R   10 W N C S L S

Odd One Out

Which one of these pictures is the odd one out?

1

2

3

4

5

Scramble TIME

Which mountains and volcanoes can be forged from each of these sets of scrambled letters?

1 NEAT

2 I, A SIN?

3 NODS NOW

4 SEER VET

5 MY NICKEL

6 THREAT NORM

7 ARK AT OAK

8 MINK OIL AJAR

Four by Four TIME

How quickly can you solve this mini crossword?

	1	2	3	4
5				
6				
7				

ACROSS

1 Decorative ribbons
5 Egg-shaped
6 Pool, lake
7 Reared

DOWN

1 Military shell
2 Above
3 Pottery goods
4 Snow vehicle

Honeycomb

TIME

Write the six-letter answers clockwise round their respective cell-numbers, starting at the arrowed cell. On completion, you will find that the unclued answers (10 and 11) will reveal **an item of sports equipment**.

1 Yearbook
2 Last movement of a symphony
3 Tasty scrap of food
4 Nut used for making marzipan
5 Fine white china clay
6 Cricket stumps
7 Young cat
8 Be present at
9 Soup bowl

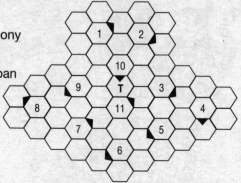

Mind the Gap

TIME

Can you complete the five words in each set by adding the same three-letter word? For example OUR in HLY, VIG, FTH (hourly, vigour, fourth), and so on.

1 ENTE HOODK PERIKLE RED SAG

2 DEMATION LENIST MH PEL SASM

3 AGE CAUAY ELHERE PRAIORTHY ROOOD

4 BUDS FIDED GADRY MANOUT VEABLE

5 ELES IILITY OBS RUOUT WANE

Missing Link

TIME

The three words in each clue have a fourth word in common, and that's your answer. For example, the clue 'Moon • Navy • Royal' gives the answer BLUE (blue moon, navy blue, royal blue). Write each answer in the grid, and the shaded column will reveal a weather feature.

1 Bowler • Keep • Maker **1**

2 Jay • Moon • Over **2**

3 Cooker • Go • Worm **3**

4 Cream • Dough • Grapes **4**

5 Low • Mark • Yule **5**

Mini Jigsaw

Fit the pieces in the grid to spell out a building in each row.

Killer Sudoku

TIME

The normal rules of Sudoku apply. Place a digit from 1-9 in each empty square so that each row, column and 3x3 block contains all the digits from 1-9. In addition, the digits in each inner shape (marked by dots) must add up to the number in the top corner of that box. No digit can be repeated within an inner shape.

WORKOUT 159

Number Jig

All but one of these numbers will fit in the grid. How quickly can you get the numbers placed?

3 Digits	4380	5 Digits
~~120~~	4523	13531
141	4621	13581
149	5522	18531
174	5555	61293
259	5596	81495
333	5698	93539
	7698	
4 Digits	7755	**7 Digits**
1163	7913	1236789
1220	8423	1239876
1771	9142	
2183		
3516		

Mini Fit

Which one of the listed words won't fit in each of these mini grids?

ARM
BYE
MET
RUB
TIN

AND
DOG
GEL
GIN
OLD

DEAR
IDOL
LAIR
LARD
ROAD

ANEW
CLAW
CODE
FEED
TALC

Elimination

TIME

All but two of the listed words fall into one of the four categories.
Put these leftover words together, and what word or phrase do they make?

CATEGORIES Adverbs • Young animals • Hats • SLEEP synonyms

Well	Hot	Kid	Head	Cloche	Snooze
Nap	Greedily	Slumber	Kip	Calf	Happily
Topper	Trilby	Fast	Puppy	Much	
Lamb	Doze	Chick	Bowler	Mitre	

Fare's Fair

TIME

Find two words of the same sound but different spelling to satisfy each two-element clue, then decide which of the pair goes where in the grid to discover **a punctuation mark**, reading down the arrowed column.

Saw the panorama

Herds of flowers

Joins the wild cat

Certain by the sea

Orchestra prohibited

Correct procedure

Set Square

TIME

Place one each of the digits 1-9 in the grid to make the sums work. We've put in some of the numbers to start you off. Sums should be solved from left to right, or from top to bottom.

Wordsearch

How quickly can you find the five themed words in each grid?

COURT

S	G	L	C	S	P	D
O	S	J	U	D	G	E
R	J	E	W	I	L	X
Z	U	U	N	A	B	J
T	R	K	I	T	V	A
H	Y	R	M	E	I	Y
F	T	K	C	O	D	W

SHOES

L	O	A	F	E	R	E
P	J	M	E	P	S	V
X	D	Y	U	B	M	O
G	F	M	G	L	I	T
R	P	F	O	O	E	K
W	N	A	R	Q	L	E
H	L	Z	B	U	C	C

Copycats

Choose the answer that best copies the pattern.

SIR is to RISK as NIL is to: Kiln • Milk • Line • Lain • Link

12 is to 3 as 16 is to: 5 • 6 • 7 • 8 • 9

OCTOPUS is to INK as SCORPION is to: Tail • Pen • Sting • Desert • Sign

DATE is to LATE as EAST is to: West • Mast • Past • Vast • Best

FLOOR is to FLOUR as BREAD is to: Dough • Bream • Knead • Breed • Wheat

Cell Blocks

			4	
5			4	4
	3	2		
		1	2	
		5		
3			3	

Fill the grid by drawing blocks along the gridlines. Each block must be square or rectangular and must contain the number of squares indicated by the digit inside it. Each block must contain only one digit.

Sudoku TIME

Place a number in each empty square so that each row, each column and each 2x2 block contains all the numbers from 1-4.

	2	1	
1			2
2			3
	3	2	

4			3
		4	
3			2

2		3	4
3			2

Add Up TIME

If the number in each circle is the sum of the two below it, how quickly can you figure out the top number? Try this one in your head, before writing anything down.

TIME [ ]

Codeword

Can you crack the code and fill in the crossword grid? Each letter of the alphabet makes at least one appearance in the grid, and is represented by the same number wherever it appears. The four letters we've decoded should help you to identify other letters and words in the grid.

Codeword grid (top row includes decoded letters F L A T):

	10	5	12 (F)	7 (L)	26 (A)	17 (T)	17	8	15	11	5	18
26		26		26		8		2		24		15
21	8	11	16	10	15	8		8	7	26	17	8
21		1		23		17		25		18		19
26	14	8	23		19	8	26	17	3	8	15	
10		7		17		15		11				18
7	26	13	24	26	5		24	9	3	26	11	15
17				14		12		5		20		8
	21	17	26	4	7	8	15		20	10	11	5
6		26		26		8		1		26		26
11	17	25	3	13		22	7	26	21	17	8	23
19		11		8		7		5		11		8
11	5	17	8	15	12	8	15	8	5	25	8	

A ~~B~~ C D E ~~F~~ G H I J K ~~L~~ M N O P Q R S ~~T~~ U V W X Y Z

1	2	3	4	5	6	7 (L)	8	9	10	11	12 (F)	13
14	15	16	17 (T)	18	19	20	21	22	23	24	25	26 (A)

Spot the Sum

TIME [ ]

In each of these boxes, one of the numbers is the sum of two others. Can you spot the sum?

1

16 8 3 27 34
23 10 9 14

2

8 11 20 16 13
18 4 6 23

3

19 17 4 12 24
18 9 25 14

4

26 11 1 36 32
5 19 9 13 29

Memory Jog

Spend two minutes memorising this list of twenty words, then see how many of them you can recall on a separate piece of paper in another two minutes.

INFERIOR	CERTAIN	CLOAK	MEMORY
CARDBOARD	TRANSIENCE	SPRIG	SENSATION
SUCCESS	MERMAID	WAND	HORRIBLE
HAMMERHEAD	RHUBARB	NOMAD	POUR
NOW	KNEE	OMELETTE	LOGISTICS

Pieceword

With the help of the Across clues only, can you fit the 16 pieces into their correct positions in the empty grid (which, when completed, will exhibit a symmetrical pattern)?

TIME

ACROSS

1 Crucial time

2 Orange vegetable

3 Nauseate, disgust

4 Abdominal rupture

5 Most savage

6 American cooking measure

7 Revolved, rotated

8 Drawing room

9 Disregard, neglect

10 Concerning plants

11 Elongated cream cake

12 Tolerate, bear

WORKOUT 165

Futoshiki

Fill the blank squares so that each row and column contains all the numbers 1, 2 and 3. Use the given numbers and the symbols that tell you if the number in the square is larger (>) or smaller (<) than the number next to it.

Splits

Can you rearrange each of these sets of letter blocks into a word?

1 GU MER IN ES

2 RI AN HIS TO

3 LE RIG RO MA

4 NI LE LY ENT

5 PA CH AR TRI

Disavowel

Can you complete this puzzle by adding all the vowels?
There are **12 As, 7 Es, 9 Is, 11 Os and 6 Us** in the puzzle.

	R		L		J		P			L
R		C		T		L		R		
G		T					C		R	S
	D				N	C		T		
N		R		N	D		P		L	
	B		S	T		R		R		N
R		M	P		C		N		P	
H				M		L		D		C
	N	D				L			N	
N				G			S	T		L
	K		P			R			L	M

Fitword

TIME

When all of the listed words have been placed
correctly in the grid, which one is left over?

3 letters
Cur
Eat
Ire
Lot
Roe
Tug
Use
Was

4 letters
Acid
Soya
Zest

5 letters
Check
Chino
Dated
Eight
Liked

Newly
~~Venom~~
Virus

7 letters
Battler
Torrent

8 letters
Gullible
Optimist

Shape Up

TIME

Can you arrange these five-letter shapes into their correct
positions in the grid so that **ten composers** read down the columns?

173

WORKOUT 167

Pathfinder TIME

Beginning with MOSEY, and moving up, down, left or right, one letter at a time, can you trace a path of 21 ways of walking?

T	Y	A	H	S	E	D	O	T	R	E
R	D	T	S	A	L	D	E	E	P	D
E	N	I	P	I	N	K	R	C	M	N
K	U	O	T	L	H	S	L	E	E	A
B	O	E	P	S	U	F	F	Y	R	A
R	E	P	M	S	E	C	N	E	B	M
A	M	L	I	T	E	F	U	S	L	E
U	B	P	O	R	K	L	O	O	M	S
L	O	M	L	H	I	W	H	C	R	T
A	T	S	L	K	L	A	E	M	A	R
T	E	S	C	U	T	T	L	E	D	I

Spot the Sum

In each of these boxes, one of the numbers is the sum of two others. Can you spot the sum?

1

29 12 16 7 10
37 23 1 21

2

8 27 34 25 5
4 10 16 23

Opposites Attract

Can you sort each set of letter blocks into two words with opposite meanings?

1 OW AD FO LE LL

2 LE LF UB HA DO

3 VE TI SS PA IVE AC

4 ACT EX TR RE ND TE

5 BE ED IO LL IE RE NT OB US

174

Dominoes

TIME

Solve the clues then write the six-letter answers into the dominoes. You must work out whether each word fits in clockwise or anticlockwise, so that the connecting letters of the dominoes all match up.

1 ___ Anderson, *Baywatch* star
2 ___ Garden, one of *The Goodies*
3 ___ Hawn, US actress, star of *Private Benjamin*
4 ___ Wesker, playwright
5 ___ Little, film cartoon mouse
6 ___ Clarke, *Downtown* singer

Sudoku

TIME

Use your powers of reasoning to place numbers in the grid, so that each row, each column and each 3x3 block contains the numbers 1-9.

							3	
			6	2			1	7
1	4				7	8	6	
9				2	4	5		
	3	6						
2				9	3	1		
5	6				8	3	4	
			1	5			9	2
						5		

Codewords

TIME

If **DECK is 1234** and **PORT is 5678**, how quickly can you work out these shipping words? You should identify more letters as you go along.

1 1 6 3 4
2 3 7 2 9
3 4 2 2 10
4 11 6 10 1
5 7 12 1 12 7

WORKOUT 169

Number Jig TIME

Which one of the listed numbers won't fit in each of these mini grids?

192
297
298
871
917

256
364
432
546
635

2407
4867
6402
7028
9602

3094
5034
5127
5305
7942

Wordsearch TIME

Hidden in this wordsearch grid are fifteen seaside words.

V	S	R	E	I	P	C	O	W
D	J	H	U	H	R	E	T	E
N	O	S	E	A	W	E	E	D
A	S	O	B	L	K	R	L	A
S	L	P	W	C	L	E	K	P
A	L	E	U	T	W	G	I	S
L	U	B	N	O	F	C	F	U
P	G	B	T	C	N	I	Z	R
M	X	L	T	I	I	Q	R	F
S	B	E	C	D	U	N	E	D
Y	D	S	E	N	Y	O	R	G

TIME

Letter Sequence

What letter should replace the question mark in these sequences?

1 A, F, C, H, E, ?

2 X, V, S, O, J, ?

3 M, O, K, Q, I, ?, G

4 O, T, T, F, F, S, ?, E, N

5 A, C, D, G, I, ?, P, U

Wild Words

What well-known phrases and expressions are suggested by these word pictures?

❶ **AGEBEAUTY** ❷ ❸ E H T N O ❹ **FULL**

Smart Sums

Try to avoid writing down anything but the final answers to these calculations… no counting on fingers allowed either!

1. Minutes in an hour – syllables in PENELOPE
2. Days in 2 weeks + consonants in STANDARD
3. Vowels in VACUUM x sides on an octagon
4. Decades in a century ÷ syllables in CHRISTMAS
5. Different letters in PROCESSOR x players in a sextet

Kakuro

Simple addition and a bit of logical thinking will solve this one. You must write a digit in each white square so that the digits in each across section add up to the total in the triangle to the left, and the digits in each column add up to the total in the triangle above. 1-9 are the only digits to use and, although you may find a digit repeated in a row, it must not be repeated in the same section. We've solved one section for you.

Arroword

TIME

Just follow the arrows to write your answers in the grid. A handful of anagram clues will get you thinking differently.

Second-hand vehicle (4,3) ▼		Com-mercials, in short ▼		Little waves on water	▼	___ Cox, Radio 1 DJ	Squidgy item for the bath	Loathes	▼
Related but minor point or topic (4,5) ►						▼	▼		
DAD (anag)		DEAR (anag)		Mush ►				Plant pip	
►			▼	Burst	SPORE (anag) ►			▼	
Mushroom top ►			▼		Narrow roads ►				
Came up						Obtain, acquire ►			
Salesperson ►				Toboggans ►					

Small Change

TIME

Can you change one letter of each of these words to make five new words with a common theme?

1 GRILL • HAMPER • DRENCH • SEW • PLACE

2 GAVEL • BACK • BIDET • HANDED • BRAHMA

3 SHUTTER • STASH • BREAD • KNAP • TRACK

4 STARE • CERTAIN • PLAN • FAST • NODS

Futoshiki

TIME

Fill the blank squares so that each row and column contains all the numbers 1, 2 and 3. Use the given numbers and the symbols that tell you if the number in the square is larger (>) or smaller (<) than the number next to it.

Fix Six

TIME

The six **birds** listed will fit into this pattern of six adjoining hexagons. All are entered clockwise from a triangle to be discovered. Adjoining triangles always contain the same letter. The **P** gives you a start.

CURLEW   SHRIKE

FALCON   THRUSH

PETREL   TOUCAN

Mobile Code

TIME

If HAIR is 4247 on this phone keypad, what other things that can be knotted have the following numbers?

1	2 ABC	3 DEF
4 GHI	5 JKL	6 MNO
7 PQRS	8 TUV	9 WXYZ
*	0	#

1 843

2 787464

3 742266

4 268866

5 7866224

Four by Four

TIME

How quickly can you solve these mini crosswords?

1	2	3	4
5			
6			
7			

ACROSS
1 Bottle stopper
5 Word ending a prayer
6 Heap (of papers, eg)
7 Eye swelling

DOWN
1 Peaked hats
2 Leave out
3 Depend (upon)
4 Leg joint

WORKOUT 173

Spot the Sum

In each of these boxes, one of the numbers is the sum of two others. Can you spot the sum?

1

9   5   29   32   18
13   21   6   25

2

8   13   27   25   1
16   29   6   32

Splits

Can you rearrange each of these sets of letter blocks into a word?

1 BO IGH LE BS

2 SA NT GE NEW

3 AN EV CE GRI

4 NU DO TS UGH

5 LY NE RAL UT

Take Five

The three answers in this mini-crossword read the same across and down. We've clued the three answers, but not in the right order. See how quickly you can solve it.

Deadly

Creek

Civilian dress

Mini Jigsaw

Fit the pieces in the grid to spell out a river in each row.

Killer Sudoku

The normal rules of Sudoku apply. Place a digit from 1-9 in each empty square so that each row, column and 3x3 block contains all the digits from 1-9. In addition, the digits in each inner shape (marked by dots) must add up to the number in the top corner of that box. No digit can be repeated within an inner shape.

WORKOUT 175

Logical TIME

Try solving this little logical problem in your head before putting pen to paper.

Three friends met up at a Halloween fancy dress party. If Larry, not dressed as Dracula, arrived after Harry who, being a poseur, turned up as Tarzan, and Superman arrived before Dracula, when did Barry arrive and in which costume?

Staircase TIME

When the seven **terms from the film industry** are correctly placed along the horizontal rows, the letters in the diagonal "staircase" will yield an eighth.

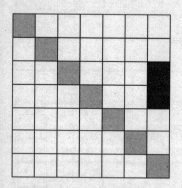

BIOPIC   FILM SET   X-RATED

BIT PART   MONTAGE

COSTUME   OUT-TAKE

Word Builder TIME

Using the nine letters provided, can you answer these clues? Every answer musts include the highlighted letter B. Which standard use all nine letters?

5 Letters

Fossilised resin

Pair

Fracture

Park seat

Bread producer

Detox therapy

6 Letters

Supporter

Financier

Tree part

Set out on a journey

Road surface curve

Transgression (of a confidence, eg)

7 Letters

Room

Tall coarse fern

Opposites Attract

Can you sort each set of letter blocks into two words with opposite meanings?

1 RK HT DA LIG

2 FO TER AF BE RE

3 ED OUD ASH PR AM

4 SE FI RE AR NED CO

Set Square

Place one each of the digits 1-9 in the grid to make the sums work. We've put in some of the numbers to start you off. Sums should be solved from left to right, or from top to bottom.

	+		−		= 9
+		+		X	
	−		+		= 8
÷		÷		÷	
	+		÷	3	= 3

= 4   = 2   = 2

In and Out

Without changing the order of the letters, add or remove one letter each time to leave a (different) new complete word and put the added or removed letters in their respective boxes to find **another name for the harmonica** reading down the boxes.

TRAP		POUT	
SCOUT		GRAPE	
ROE		TIGER	
METRE		WHET	
BATED		BRIE	

Wordsearch

TIME

How quickly can you find the five themed words in each grid?

HISTORY

W	S	K	X	M	O	H
I	Y	T	B	A	A	K
N	Z	W	U	N	I	R
D	H	F	O	A	U	O
S	P	V	N	R	R	Y
O	E	R	O	D	U	T
R	D	T	C	L	G	Q

GEOGRAPHY

C	T	L	C	N	D	W
R	X	O	I	H	E	F
J	U	S	T	I	S	Y
V	A	S	C	A	E	M
B	Q	N	R	G	R	K
P	K	R	A	P	T	E
T	L	E	B	D	B	Z

Three in One

TIME

The three parts of each clue lead to the same answer word. Can you solve any before you reach the third part?

1   Left • Type of wine • Harbour
2   Wolf • Scarper • Door-lock
3   Guard duty • Observe • Timepiece
4   Jalopy • Firework • Sausage
5   Lucifer • Coincide • Football game

Cell Blocks

TIME

Fill the grid by drawing blocks along the gridlines. Each block must be square or rectangular and must contain the number of squares indicated by the digit inside it. Each block must contain only one digit.

Sudoku   TIME

Place a number in each empty square so that each row, each column and each 2x2 block contains all the numbers from 1-4.

Add Up   TIME

If the number in each circle is the sum of the two below it, how quickly can you figure out the top number? Try this one in your head, before writing anything down.

Codeword

TIME ____

Can you crack the code and fill in the crossword grid? Each letter of the alphabet makes at least one appearance in the grid, and is represented by the same number wherever it appears. The four letters we've decoded should help you to identify other letters and words in the grid.

23		23		21		4		6		25	
9	8	25	11	7		3	7	10	2	23	9	11
23		7		10		8		18		19		26
11	15	11	25	13	11	14		16	18	10	13	23
4			11		11			18		19		20
13	23	9	1		2	7	11	11	5	8	9	20
17		11		3				13		12		11
11	16	18	23	12	12	11	14		22	11	11	7
13		7		23		8		20				23
8	7	10	9	24 (Y)		20	23	7	19	11	9	13
4		13		3 (P)		17		23		23		8
11	22	8	14	11 (E)	9	13		2	10	7	20	10
	25		9 (N)		24		13		12		9	

A B C D E̸ F G H I J K L M N̸ O P̸ Q R S T U V W X X̸ Z

1	2	3 P	4	5	6	7	8	9 N	10	11 E	12	13
14	15	16	17	18	19	20	21	22	23	24 Y	25	26

So Complete

TIME ____

Complete each trio of words with a common letter. The five letters will form the answer word. Where there is a choice of completing letter, you must decide which is needed.

I_LE	LEN_	BAR_	☐
T_RN	POL_	_VER	☐
LA_E	_EAL	JA_Z	☐
B_AR	CH_W	HER_	☐
TOW_	SCA_	AC_E	☐

Memory Jog

Give yourself two minutes to memorise this list of thirty words. How many of them can you recall on a separate piece of paper in another two minutes?

PHOBIA	CUSHION	SPORT	LOCKET
FRIENDLY	WILLOW	RIPPLE	DUMB-BELL
ATTITUDE	SANDAL	CHARIOT	FIN
CLEARLY	COUGHING	BUCKLE	DARING
EXPECT	FORTUNATE	TALL	MAYONNAISE
DECISION	SCRATCH	BEADS	CRUMBLE
MOOR	QUEASY	SHRILL	
SWORD	DANGLE	DIGITAL	

Number Jig

TIME

All but one of these numbers will fit in the grid.
How quickly can you get the numbers placed?

3 Digits
287
359
387
633
~~833~~
839

4 Digits
1312
1452
2518
2649
3434

3441
3443
3649
4512
4538
4542
5438
5563
6434
6448
9827
9842

5 Digits
25428
25437
28231
28321
33157
33257

7 Digits
3456543
5432345

187

WORKOUT 181

Scramble TIME

What birds can be made from each of these sets of scrambled letters?

1 LOW
2 SO EGO
3 PINE GUN
4 OF CLAN
5 RANG LIST
6 HEAT SNAP
7 SALT BOARS
8 WE ROPE DOCK

Initials TIME

If ITHOTN (Oscar-winning film) is *IN THE HEAT OF THE NIGHT*, what do these initials represent?

1 SOL (American landmark)
2 LOTV (Flower)
3 TMOV (Shakespeare play)
4 PIB (Rolling Stones song)
5 KCS (Breed of dog)

Honeycomb TIME

Write the six-letter answers clockwise round their respective cell-numbers, starting at the arrowed cell. On completion, you will find that the unclued answers (10 and 11) will reveal **a three-word phrase meaning "at no cost."**

1 Previously
2 Elevenses drink
3 Spidery, untidy handwriting
4 Bull's noise
5 Look for diligently
6 Photographer's instrument
7 Thin
8 Sleep intermittently – like puss?
9 Repudiate

188

Fitword

TIME

When all of the listed words have been placed correctly in the grid, which one is left over?

3 letters

Flu
Imp
Ink
Via

4 letters

Gang
Smut

5 letters

Evict
~~Mufti~~
Nymph
Taken

7 letters

Needier
Plateau

8 letters

Butchery
Cheering
Narrator
Splicing
Thuggery

11 letters

Interacting

M U F T I

Mini Jigsaw

TIME

Fit the pieces in the grid to spell out the name of a writer in each row.

WORKOUT 183

Pathfinder TIME

Beginning with RAMSAY MACDONALD, and moving up, down, left or right, one letter at a time, can you trace a path of fifteen British Prime Ministers?

Q	S	A	O	S	L	I	W	N	U	O
U	O	N	N	M	I	L	L	A	G	D
I	T	A	M	C	A	M	O	H	L	E
T	S	J	O	L	O	E	M	S	A	E
H	R	E	R	L	Y	L	A	T	T	L
A	L	M	E	G	D	E	E	P	L	A
P	N	R	O	C	D	O	N	E	P	W
W	I	G	E	A	M	L	A	L	O	N
D	E	R	E	A	Y	D	E	D	E	I
L	Y	G	L	R	A	A	H	C	N	A
A	B	R	A	M	S	M	B	E	R	L

Number Jig TIME

Which one of the listed numbers won't fit in each of these mini grids?

137
267
417
724
737

157
351
357
371
713

2935
3949
5229
5392
9235

Pairs TIME

Pair off 24 of the listed words to form twelve "double-barrelled" words and rearrange the letters of the two words left over to reveal **a medicinal preparation**.

APPLE	CUSTARD	HARD	PIANO	SWITCH
BEST	EGG	LIGHT	PLATES	TITLE
BOILED	FIGHT	MASTER	POWER	
BOY	FRIEND	MOSS	SCHOOL	
CHEESE	GLASSES	NIGHT	STATION	
COURTESY	GRAND	OPERA	SUNDAY	

Manor Born

TIME

Which numbered photo has been taken?

Sudoku

TIME

Use your powers of reasoning to place numbers in the grid, so that each row, each column and each 3x3 block contains the numbers 1-9.

		6					9	8
		5	4	7		1		
1						7	2	
8			5	1	3			
	3							
4			7	9	6			
9						2	7	
		2	6	8		4		
		4					5	9

Splits

TIME

Can you rearrange each of these sets of letter blocks into a word?

1 MAT AU IC TO

2 RY SE TA CRE

3 TU AL NOC RN

4 VE BLE TA GE

5 LY AR QU TER

WORKOUT 185

Word Builder

Using the nine letters provided, can you answer these clues? Every answer must include the highlighted letter L. Which piece of exercise equipment uses all nine letters?

L I D
E L M
T A R

5 Letters
Volume measurement
Wide awake
Roofer
River mouth
Afterwards
Perfect

6 Letters
Sell
Posted
Wooden hammer
Ring again
Small particular
Corn grinder

7 Letters
Word for word, to the letter
Followed
Agreed

8 Letters
Tested

Wordsearch

Hidden in this wordsearch grid are fifteen chocolate words.

Z	B	M	Q	K	Y	Z	W	E
C	H	O	I	C	E	R	F	T
M	U	E	N	L	A	A	U	I
A	I	U	N	P	K	E	D	H
E	T	F	P	I	D	R	G	W
R	C	E	G	W	L	E	E	T
C	R	O	J	O	E	A	F	L
D	S	H	F	F	V	O	R	M
A	T	A	F	F	S	X	C	P
R	X	O	B	R	E	Y	A	L
K	T	M	E	N	U	E	P	N

Codewords

If **BEACH is 12345** and **SHORE is 65782**, how quickly can you work out these beach words? You should identify more letters as you go along.

1 6 2 3

2 4 8 3 1

3 4 7 3 6 9

4 8 2 6 7 8 9

5 1 3 9 5 2 8 6

Memory Jog

Give yourself two minutes to memorise this list of words –
twenty-five this time! How many of them can you recall on
a separate piece of paper in another two minutes?

MIGHT	TABLE	BELL	ORCHESTRA	SHEEP
CUPBOARD	RAIN	SHIPYARD	POLITE	WALL
ICING	FORWARD	EVENLY	BEHIND	MAJORITY
PLAICE	REVENGE	MASK	GREEN	PADDLE
SINCERTITY	TONE	WANDER	DUSTY	REMINDER

Small Change

Can you change one letter of each of these words to make five
new words with a common theme?

1 DIRE • DANGER • SPEAK • MALE • CLUE

2 BIN • BARGE • BRAND • VASE • HUGS

3 MANGE • TEXT • BASIS • BUTTON • TAP

4 SPINE • NAME • ATTAR • CREPT • SEW

Kakuro

Simple addition and a bit of logical thinking will solve this one. You must write
a digit in each white square so that the digits in each across section add up to
the total in the triangle to the left, and the digits in each column add up to the
total in the triangle above. 1-9 are the only digits to use and, although you may
find a digit repeated in a row, it must not be repeated in the same section.
We've solved one section for you.

WORKOUT 187

Arroword

Just follow the arrows to write your answers in the grid. A handful of anagram clues will get you thinking differently.

	▼	Letters after a firm's name (abbr)	▼	___ Norman, golfer	▼	Part of cauliflower or broccoli	▼	Give extra vigour or spirit to	Very much (4,2)
TAILED (anag)									
Conflict (with)							▼		▼
Sharp poke		BARS (anag)		2003 Will Ferrell film ▶				Theatre in Dublin	
▶			▼	Large antelope	Narrow valley ▶			▼	
Family ___, genealogy chart			▼		Bring up (young) ▶				
▶				Undershirts ▶					
Cure	Mr Blue ___, ELO hit			___ Walcott, Arsenal player ▶					

Scramble

The names of which type of dining venue can be made from each of these sets of scrambled letters? I think this calls for a cream cake!

1 RAB

2 NIN

3 FACE

4 ROBS IT

5 EAR YET

6 NEAR VAT

7 SHYER LOT

8 BRAISE RES

Initials

If **ITHOTN** (Oscar-winning film) is *IN THE HEAT OF THE NIGHT*, what do these initials represent?

1 OFITG (Sitcom)

2 WAM (Composer)

3 HAS (Children's game)

4 YOLT (Bond film)

5 ASITSN (Proverb)

Mini Fit

Which one of the listed words won't fit in each of these mini grids?

ANT
ART
NAG
ROT
TOR

DEN
END
PEN
PET
PIE

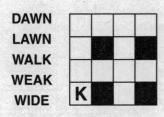

DAWN
LAWN
WALK
WEAK
WIDE

ELSE
SEEN
SLOW
SWAT
TWIN

Vowel Play

Can you replace the missing vowels to complete the names of these musical instruments?

1 V L N
2 T R M P T
3 G T R
4 C C R D N
5 P N

6 B
7 B S S N
8 F L T
9 R G N
10 C L L

Set Square

Place one each of the digits 1-9 in the grid to make the sums work. We've put in some of the numbers to start you off. Sums should be solved from left to right, or from top to bottom.

WORKOUT 189

Spot the Sum

In each of these boxes, one of the numbers is the sum of two others. Can you spot the sum?

1
21 4 30 16 10
24 7 27 8

3
2 21 38 33 13
3 26 9 22

2
26 14 11 1 6
29 22 4 19

4
22 7 44 33 35
18 21 12 27

Box Wise

 TIME

Can you place the three-letter groups in the boxes, so that neighbouring boxes always make a six-letter word, like PAR-DON or DON-ATE? We've placed one group to start you off.

PER

CER	ISE	~~PER~~	SUP
CON	MAN	RES	TRA
EAL	MIT	SHA	ULT

Staircase

 TIME

When the seven **TV programmes** are correctly placed along the horizontal rows, the letters in the diagonal "staircase" will yield an eighth.

ANGELS

FRASIER

HI-DE-HI!

MR BEAN

POP IDOL

SPENDER

TAGGART

196

Mini Jigsaw

Fit the pieces in the grid to spell out a part of a car in each row.

Six Pack

Can you place digits in the empty triangles, so that the numbers in each hexagon add up to 25? Only single digits between 1 and 9 can be used, and no two numbers in any hexagon may be the same.

197

SOLUTIONS

WORKOUT 1
WORDSEARCH

R	I	G	J	L	C	F		E	L	P	P	A	P	F
R	I	A	L	C	E	V		P	N	A	B	Y		T
X	Z	T	S	E	Y	E		F	A	W	A	G	E	L
N	T	E	P	M	N	Q		Z	S	P	N	J	X	B
D	A	A	B	O	U	B		R	G	R	A	P	E	M
U	G	U	C	W	B	O		C	U	Q	N	I	K	
W	K	S	T	A	R	T		H	V	O	A	G	A	D

SPLITS
1 Discovery **2** Tolerated
3 Solicitor **4** Longitude
5 Whichever

CELL BLOCKS

WORKOUT 2
SUDOKU

3	4	2	1
2	1	4	3
4	3	1	2
1	2	3	4

2	4	1	3
1	3	2	4
4	1	3	2
3	2	4	1

3	4	2	1
1	2	4	3
4	1	3	2
2	3	1	4

ADD UP
1 48 **2** 35 **3** 26

WORKOUT 3
CODEWORD

SPOT THE SUM
1 33 (14+19) **2** 33 (12+21)
3 21 (3+18) **4** 34 (6+28)

WORKOUT 4
PYRAMID
1 I **2** It **3** Tie **4** Tier
5 Inert **6** Retina **7** Terrain
8 Restrain **9** Arresting

WORKOUT 5
FUTOSHIKI

1	3	2	4

3	4	1	2

2	1	4	3

4	2	3	1

INITIALS
1 *When I'm Cleaning
Windows* **2** *Three Blind
Mice* **3** Steak and kidney
pie **4** *The Lion, The Witch
and the Wardrobe* **5** Red
lorry, yellow lorry

TOWN TO TOWN
CROYDON
1 Condor **2** Rondo **3** Door
4 Rod **5** Road **6** Adorn
7 Roland
ORLANDO

WORKOUT 6
FITWORD

L	I	M	P		P	A	I	R
U		E		E		O		O
C	U	D		M	E	R	I	T
K		I		U		T		U
	J	A	W		S	A	W	N
O		E		G		O		D
B	O	M	B		W	A	X	
T		I		G		R		D
A	N	N	O	Y		O	W	E
I		U		M		M		F
N	E	S	T		Z	A	N	Y

Leftover word: **HIT**

SIX PACK

WORKOUT 7
PATHFINDER

E	D	L	E	C	I	T	I	V	H	A
U	E	K	I	U	O	N	A	E	L	I
T	Z	E	B	S	J	J	H	R	E	M
E	R	J	O	A	H	O	S	E	J	H
N	O	L	A	B	A	U	H	M	I	A
O	I	E	K	K	J	G	E	S	C	I
M	N	E	K	U	U	D	M	E	A	D
Y	A	X	O	A	H	A	N	H	A	
N	D	H	D	N	A	H	T	O	B	
A	H	A	U	S	Z	E	P	A	T	I
M	U	I	M	E	H	E	N	S	N	O

NUMBER JIG
1 324 **2** 469 **3** 3131

COPYCATS
1 Speak **2** Drey **3** Caddy
4 Mule (change the 2nd
letter to the 6th after it in
the alphabet)

WORKOUT 8
DOMINOES
1 Marina 2 Bernie 3 Albert
4 Teresa 5 Creole 6 Arnold

SUDOKU

8	3	6	9	2	1	4	5	7
5	9	4	3	6	7	8	2	1
2	7	1	4	5	8	6	9	3
3	8	9	5	1	6	2	7	4
1	2	7	8	3	4	5	6	9
6	4	5	2	7	9	3	1	8
4	6	3	7	9	2	1	8	5
9	1	8	6	4	5	7	3	2
7	5	2	1	8	3	9	4	6

CODEWORDS
1 Charm (of finches)
2 Crash (of rhinoceroses)
3 Swarm (of bees)
4 Murder (of crows)
5 Pride (of lions) (8=C,
9=S, 10=W, 11=U, 12=P,
13=I)

WORKOUT 9

MINI FIT
1 Tic 2 Rod 3 Five 4 Erne

WORDSEARCH

Banjo, Cello, Clarinet, Cymbals, Drums, Flute, Gong, Guitar, Harp, Oboe, Piano, Piccolo, Timpani, Trombone, Trumpet, Tuba, Viola, Violin

SCRAMBLE
1 Rome 2 Paris 3 Athens
4 Copenhagen 5 Bucharest
6 Budapest 7 Amsterdam
8 Bratislava

WORKOUT 10

SMALL CHANGE
1 Ford, Rover, Fiat, Seat, Lexus 2 Rose, Daisy, Lily, Iris, Pansy 3 Gold, Silver, Tin, Iron, Lead 4 Table, Chair, Desk, Chest, Dresser

OPPOSITES ATTRACT
1 Empty/Full
2 Finish/Start
3 Difficult/Simple
4 Precise/Vague

KAKURO

	3	1		8	9		8	1
3	1	2	5	4	7	8	9	6
1	2		1	3		9	7	

WORKOUT 11

ARROWORD

	S		F		G	W	
P	R	O	M	I	S	E	F
E	G		L	E	A	V	E
W	E	B		B	A	K	E	R
C	R	I	M	E		E	R	R
C	H	I	C		R	A	N	G	E
	M	E	L	T		S	E	T

VOWEL PLAY
1 Carrot 2 Potato
3 Lettuce 4 Pea 5 Leek 6 Kale
7 Onion 8 Celery 9 Radish
10 Beetroot

SMART SUMS
1 30 (5 x 6) 2 16 (64÷4)
3 37 (50-13) 4 11 (4+7)

WORKOUT 12

EGG-TIMER
1 Hearts 2 Share 3 Rash
4 Ash 5 As 6 Sea 7 Peas
8 Spade 9 Spades

MOBILE CODE
1 Cap 2 Beret 3 Panama
4 Trilby 5 Bowler

FOUR BY FOUR

B	O	L	T
A	R	I	A
T	A	L	K
S	L	O	E

WORKOUT 13

SET SQUARE

3	+	7	−	2
−		+		×
1	+	9	−	6
×		÷		+
5	×	4	−	8

IN AND OUT
Cares (- S), cache (+ C), herd (- A), rifle (+ L), scream (+ E) **SCALE**
Rap (- M), coroner (+ O), brand (+ D), case (- E), bind (- L) **MODEL**

BOX WISE
1 Cor 2 Out 3 Set 4 Tee
5 Rep 6 Lay 7 The 8 Ory
9 Man 10 Tra 11 Nce 12 Vel

WORKOUT 14

MINI JIGSAW
Gannet, Osprey, Grouse, Oriole, Cuckoo, Plover

KILLER SUDOKU

7	2	5	8	3	1	6	9	4
1	6	3	4	9	2	8	5	7
4	8	9	6	5	7	2	1	3
6	1	2	7	4	5	3	8	9
8	3	4	2	1	9	7	6	5
9	5	7	3	8	6	1	4	2
2	7	8	5	6	4	9	3	1
5	9	6	1	2	3	4	7	8
3	4	1	9	7	8	5	2	6

WORKOUT 15

STAIRCASE
Hayrick, Arable, Farmer, Drovers, Yield, Crops, Piglet.

The word is: **HARVEST**

NUMBER SEQUENCE
1 49 (sum of previous two numbers, take away 1) 2 5 (letters in name of numbers one, two, three etc) 3 2732 (x4, -4) 4 5040 (x1, x2, x3 etc) 5 1093 (x3,+1)

WORD BUILDER
Tiger, Irate, Might, Eater, Eight, Gather, Either, Metier, Heater, Gaiter, Ragtime, Meatier, Emirate, Emigrate, Heritage, Hermitage

SOLUTIONS

WORKOUT 16
WILD WORDS
1 Think twice **2** Rock around the clock **3** Hole in one **4** Broad bean

FARE'S FAIR

R	O	S	E	
C	H	E	C	K
M	A	R	E	
W	R	I	T	E
	S	A	W	
T	O	L	D	

ELIMINATION
Dairy – Brie, Cheese, Milk, Whey, Yogurt.
HAND – Cuff, Made, Set, Shake, Some.
Gases – Argon, Hydrogen, Methane, Neon, Oxygen.
Boxing – Corner, Gloves, Ring, Ropes, Spar.

Leftover phrase: **WELL DONE**

WORKOUT 17
NINERS
Telescope, worldwide, inelegant, gondolier
The left-hand column gives **TWIG**.

CELL BLOCKS

	4			4
3			1	
	4		4	
	4		2	6
		4		

WORKOUT 18
SUDOKU

4	2	3	1
3	1	4	2
1	4	2	3
2	3	1	4

2	3	1	4
1	4	2	3
3	1	4	2
4	2	3	1

4	2	3	1
3	1	4	2
2	3	1	4
1	4	2	3

ADD UP
1 38 **2** 42 **3** 48

WORKOUT 19
CODEWORD

COPY CATS
1 Open **2** Sun **3** PQRS (1st letter to 4th) **4** Drive **5** Taps (reorder letters into new positions)

WORKOUT 20
SPLITS
1 Beefsteak **2** Unlimited **3** Redundant **4** Signature **5** Godmother

SHAPE UP

R	T	G	S	B	R	I	T	R	S
O	U	I	T	R	E	N	I	U	I
T	R	O	U	A	N	G	T	B	S
H	N	T	B	Q	O	R	I	E	L
K	E	T	B	U	I	E	A	N	E
O	R	O	S	E	R	S	N	S	Y

WORKOUT 21
FUTOSHIKI

1	3	2	4
3	4	1	2
2	1	4	3
4	2	3	1

SCRAMBLE
1 Shoe **2** Spat **3** Skate **4** Gaiter **5** Brogue **6** Slipper **7** Espadrille **8** Wellington

PET TALK
Photograph 2

WORKOUT 22
FITWORD

Kitty

MIND THE GAP
Tetanus, Academy, Acrobat, Adamant, Forever, Instead, Affirms, Awaking.

The creature is:
AARDVARK

WORKOUT 23
PATHFINDER

PIRATE SHIP, TRIMARAN, SKIFF, CORACLE, PRIVATEER, CLIPPER, SLOOP, NARROWBOAT, HOUSEBOAT, FERRY, CAIQUE, BATTLESHIP, BARGE, GALLEON, DHOW, MOTORBOAT, CANOE

SOUNDALIKES
1 Threw/through **2** Poor/paw **3** Where/wear

HONEYCOMB
1 Degree **2** Drudge **3** Beware! **4** Darwin **5** Coward **6** People **7** Pulpit **8** Hamper **9** Lumber **10&11** George Orwell

200

WORKOUT 24

SET SQUARE

9	×	2	−	1
+		×		+
7	+	8	÷	5
−		÷		+
3	×	4	−	6

SUDOKU

8	2	3	9	1	4	5	6	7
6	9	4	7	8	5	3	1	2
5	7	1	6	2	3	8	9	4
3	5	9	4	7	2	6	8	1
4	8	7	1	3	6	2	5	9
2	1	6	5	9	8	4	7	3
7	4	2	8	5	9	1	3	6
1	3	5	2	6	7	9	4	8
9	6	8	3	4	1	7	2	5

INITIALS

1 A friend in need is a friend indeed **2** *The Old Curiosity Shop* **3** He's from Barcelona **4** *One Flew Over the Cuckoo's Nest* **5** Bread and butter pudding

WORKOUT 25

FIX SIX

WORDSEARCH

PICTURE PAIR

1 and 5

WORKOUT 26

NUMBER JIG

1 439 **2** 165 **3** 7239

SMALL CHANGE

1 Scone, Tart, Bun, Cake, Pie **2** Tarn, Lake, Pool, Pond, Mere **3** Stone, Pound, Ton, Gram, Ounce **4** Shorts, Skirt, Kilt, Gown, Dress

KAKURO

		1	7	9	2		8	9
1	2	5	9	8	3	6	4	7
3	1		4	6	1	2		

WORKOUT 27

ARROWORD

	A		S		O		M	
A	S	A	T	S	U	M	A	R
S		Y		T	E	R	S	E
J	U	T		C	L	A	M	P
	R	A	D	A	R		C	I	A
R	E	L	Y		O	V	A	L	S
	K	E	L	P		S	E	T

TAKE FIVE

T	I	B	I	A
I		A		L
B	A	N	A	L
I		A		O
A	L	L	O	W

TWO OF A KIND

1 Decent/Proper **2** Choice/Special **3** Caretaker/Janitor **4** Pinpoint/Spot **5** Impromptu/Spontaneous

WORKOUT 28

WORDSEARCH

VOWEL PLAY

1 *Doctors* **2** *Spooks* **3** *Coast* **4** *Hustle* **5** *Newsnight* **6** *Casualty* **7** *Morse* **8** *Lost* **9** *Panorama* **10** *Countdown*

THREE IN ONE

1 Score **2** Bear **3** Lay **4** Drive **5** Slide

WORKOUT 29

MISSING LINK

1 Wide **2** Star **3** Care **4** Bath **5** Test. The game is: **DARTS**

CODEWORDS

1 Eagle **2** Hole **3** Ball **4** Birdie **5** Wood **6** Wedge (9=E, 10=H, 11=B, 12=D, 13=W)

MIND THE GAP

1 Pet **2** Ore **3** Add **4** Fun **5** Dig

WORKOUT 30

MINI JIGSAW

Purple, Silver, Yellow Orange, Violet, Indigo

KILLER SUDOKU

3	6	4	5	2	7	8	1	9
1	9	7	3	8	6	2	5	4
8	5	2	1	9	4	7	6	3
2	7	6	4	3	8	1	9	5
9	8	3	6	1	5	4	2	7
5	4	1	9	7	2	6	3	8
7	3	5	2	4	1	9	8	6
6	2	8	7	5	9	3	4	1
4	1	9	8	6	3	5	7	2

SOLUTIONS

WORKOUT 31
MINI FIT
1 Tip **2** Mat **3** Tube **4** Deaf

WORD BUILDER
Teach, Scare, Chore, Chest, Chaos, Chase, Search, Actors, Caster, Corset, Coarser, Torches, Coaster, Archers, Creators, Reactors, Orchestra

WORKOUT 32
SPLITS
1 Porcupine **2** Dishonest **3** Bookplate **4** Companion **5** Smugglers. The bonus link is kitchen words within the words – Cup, Dish, Plate, Pan, Mug

PAIRS
Bank holiday, bottle-opener, campfire, cheese biscuit, cupboard, insurance claim, lemon tea, necklace, ponytail, skin-diving, squash racket, stopcock
LEANT and MOWER yield WATER MELON

WORKOUT 33
WORDSEARCH

SET SQUARE
6	−	2	+	5
×		×		+
4	×	9	÷	3
−		−		−
8	+	7	−	1

CELL BLOCKS

WORKOUT 34
SUDOKU

1	3	2	4
2	4	1	3
4	1	3	2
3	2	4	1

4	1	3	2
3	2	4	1
2	4	1	3
1	3	2	4

3	1	2	4
2	4	3	1
1	2	4	3
4	3	1	2

ADD UP
1 36
2 42
3 60

WORKOUT 35
CODEWORD

SO COMPLETE
Safe	golf,	lift	F
Pain,	pier,	chip	I
Wage,	gear,	ring	G
Ache,	chef,	heal	H
Stem,	halt,	fist	T

WORKOUT 36
SPLITS
1 Playhouse **2** Confident **3** Perishing **4** Remainder **5** Omelettes

PIECEWORD

WORKOUT 37
LETTER SEQUENCE
1 N (+3, +4, +5 etc) **2** C (-2, +1, -3, +1, -4, +1 etc) **3** M (+3, -3, -3, +3, +7, -7, -7, +7) **4** I (+10, -8, +10, -8 etc) **5** E (-1, -2, -3 etc)

MOBILE CODE
1 Bath **2** Hull **3** York **4** Leeds **5** Dundee **6** Cardiff

DISAVOWEL

WORKOUT 38
FITWORD

```
    T   S   S
URGE  ECHO
  A M   S U
SCRIPTING
  E   E   E
EDEN  DULL
  E   O
PODGINESS
  P G O I
MULL  TINT
  S E   E
```

Play

SMART SUMS
1 180 (3x60) **2** 18 (13+5) **3** 36 (4x9) **4** 60 (360÷6) **5** 8 (13-5)

202

WORKOUT 39
PATHFINDER

MARTIN, BERNARD, ALEXANDER, PAUL, LOUIS, BENEDICT, ANNE, THOMAS, ELIZABETH, LUCY, JOSEPH, HELEN, BARTHOLOMEW, THERESA, DANIEL, DAVID, PETER, FRANCIS, GABRIEL

BOX WISE
1 Mut 2 Car 3 Ton 4 Sil
5 Lea 6 Ves 7 Ver 8 Bal
9 Tal 10 Ent 11 Ity 12 Ail

LOGICAL
1st Aidan, Red Rose,
2nd Connor, Desert Dahlia,
3rd Brendan, Lilac Lilac

WORKOUT 40
SET SQUARE

4	×	6	−	8
×		+		−
9	+	1	÷	5
÷		×		+
3	×	2	+	7

SUDOKU

1	6	4	3	7	9	2	8	5
9	2	7	6	8	5	4	3	1
3	8	5	2	4	1	9	6	7
8	7	2	9	5	6	1	4	3
4	5	1	8	2	3	6	7	9
6	3	9	7	1	4	5	2	8
5	1	6	4	3	8	7	9	2
7	9	8	5	6	2	3	1	4
2	4	3	1	9	7	8	5	6

STAIRCASE
Menzies, Barclay, Scott, Ogilvy, Maxwell, Cameron, Lamond. The "staircase" reveals: MACLEOD

WORKOUT 41
MINI FIT
1 Net 2 Pip 3 Tape 4 Blur

WORD SEARCH

SCRAMBLE
1 Boxer 2 Beagle 3 Poodle
4 Pointer 5 Whippet
6 Lurcher 7 Alsatian
8 Pekinese

WORKOUT 42
NINERS
Discourse, architect, withstand, Norwegian
The left-hand column gives **DAWN**.

KAKURO

		9	3	8	1		2	1
9	8	5	1	7	2	4	6	3
7	9		6	9	4	8		

WORKOUT 43
ARROWORD

	T	R	A	F		B
G	R	E	E	N	P	A	R	T	Y
	U		V		E		A
R	E	S	E	T		A	N	T
	O	R	I	E	N	T	A	L
N	O	O	S	E		N	I	K	E
	T	E	R	R	A	C	E	D

INITIALS
1 Keep off the grass 2 *Jack and the Beanstalk* 3 Many hands make light work 4 *The Phantom of the Opera* 5 *Butch Cassidy and the Sundance Kid*

NUMBER SEQUENCE
1 26 (+1, +3, +5...) 2 60 (-10, -9, -8...) 3 34 (x2, -1, x2, -1...) 4 122 (x3-1) 5 100 (Value of British coins)

WORKOUT 44
DOMINOES
1 Rupert 2 Arthur
3 Thomas 4 Maxine
5 Joanne 6 Joseph

MOBILE CODE
1 Blue 2 Gold 3 Pink
4 Green 5 Purple

FOUR BY FOUR

C	O	O	K
U	P	O	N
F	A	Z	E
F	L	E	E

WORKOUT 45
FARE'S FAIR

	B	U	Y	E	R
S	I	G	N	E	T
	S	E	N	T	
T	H	Y	M	E	
M	O	U	R	N	
	P	L	A	C	E

FUTOSHIKI

2 1 3

3 2 1

1 3 2

STAIRCASE
Ravioli, Honey, Sausage, Hobnob, Cereal, Butter, Kebab. Edible item: RHUBARB

SOLUTIONS

WORKOUT 46

MINI JIGSAW
Fennel, Celery, Turnip
Carrot, Potato, Marrow

KILLER SUDOKU

9	5	2	7	4	8	3	6	1
4	3	1	2	9	6	5	7	8
8	6	7	1	3	5	4	2	9
6	9	5	3	8	4	2	1	7
1	8	3	9	7	2	6	5	4
7	2	4	5	6	1	9	8	3
2	7	8	4	5	9	1	3	6
3	1	9	6	2	7	8	4	5
5	4	6	8	1	3	7	9	2

WORKOUT 47

SUDOKU

3	1	2	4		2	1	3	4
4	2	1	3		4	3	2	1
2	3	4	1		1	2	4	3
1	4	3	2		3	4	1	2

3	1	4	2
2	4	1	3
4	2	3	1
1	3	2	4

WORD BUILDER
Canoe, Camel, Panic, Mince,
Clean, Pecan, Pencil, Plaice,
Cinema, Income, In place,
Pelican, Complain, Policeman

WORKOUT 48

ALPHA-FIT

SIX PACK

SPOT THE SUM
1 22 (15+7) **2** 29 (18+11)
3 30 (18+12) **4** 35 (29+6)

WORKOUT 49

ELIMINATION
Musical instruments –
Bassoon, Cornet, Cymbals,
Triangle, Viola.
PIECE – Conversation, Hair,
Master, Party, Time.
No vowels – Crypt, Lynx,
Myrrh, Rhythm, Why.
Reptiles – Alligator, Anaconda,
Cobra, Iguana, Turtle.
Leftover phrase: SQUARE
MEAL

LOGICAL
Colin, Ironing, Wednesday
Andrew, Dusting, Tuesday
Brian, Gardening, Monday

CELL BLOCKS

WORKOUT 50

WORDSEARCH

ADD UP
1 31 **2** 25 **3** 41

WORKOUT 51

CODEWORD

SOUNDALIKES
1 Caught/Court
2 Heard/Herd
3 Which/Witch
4 Knows/Nose

WORKOUT 52

SPLITS
1 Alligator **2** Xylophone
3 Sandpaper **4** Marmalade
5 Potential

SHAPE UP

B	E	H	K	F	M	G	W	K	M
A	K	A	I	A	I	R	E	I	O
C	L	R	D	R	R	A	A	N	N
A	A	L	M	R	R	B	V	S	R
L	N	O	A	O	E	L	E	K	O
L	D	W	N	W	N	E	R	I	E

WORKOUT 53

TWO OF A KIND
1 Sailor/Seaman **2** Forbid/
Prohibit **3** Conjurer/
Magician **4** Oversee/
Supervise **5** Defender/
Guardian

CODEWORDS
1 Peat **2** Potato **3** Shoots
(7=S) **4** Petal (8=L) **5** Apple

STAR TURN
Photograph 1

WORKOUT 54

FITWORD

S	I	G	H	T	S	E	E
E		R		E		M
T	I	K	K	A		E	Y	E
C		D		I	M		R
H	U	F	F	Y		I	C	Y
	U				N		
W	A	R		R	I	G	I	D
I		L	I	E			O
P	R	O		N	A	V	A	L
E		N		A		E		E
R	E	G	U	L	A	T	E

Tactile

SET SQUARE

6	÷	2	+	8
+		+		−
9	−	4	+	1
−		×		÷
5	−	3	×	7

WORKOUT 55

PATHFINDER

CHICORY, COMFREY, PARSLEY, LAVENDER, CORIANDER, MARJORAM, SAGE, GARLIC, BASIL, FENNEL, TARRAGON, OREGANO, MINT, THYME, BAY LEAVES, CHIVES, ROSEMARY, CHERVIL

PYRAMID

1 R **2** Ra **3** Era
4 Care **5** Cater **6** Trance
7 Certain **8** Canister
9 Miscreant

WORKOUT 56

MIND THE GAP

Vacancy, Gorilla, Cabbage, Acrobat, Eclipse, Twinkle, Earlier, Stencil. Musical instrument: CLARINET

SUDOKU

1	9	6	8	2	7	5	4	3
2	4	8	5	6	3	9	1	7
5	7	3	4	1	9	2	8	6
6	3	9	7	8	4	1	2	5
4	5	1	2	9	6	7	3	8
7	8	2	1	3	5	6	9	4
9	1	5	3	7	8	4	6	2
8	6	7	9	4	2	3	5	1
3	2	4	6	5	1	8	7	9

THREE IN ONE

1 Fair **2** Drive **3** Neck **4** Blue
5 Part

WORKOUT 57

MINI FIT

1 Paw **2** Cod **3** Done **4** Drop

WORD SEARCH

A	N	T	E	L	O	P	E	K
A	C	R	F	S	D	S	L	T
Z	O	A	H	P	N	E	L	R
E	W	D	R	R	V	O	E	W
N	Z	O	I	B	J	Z	R	
G	P	E	K	N	B	W	A	I
C	A	C	X	G	G	O	G	J
O	U	T	U	B	G	L	U	X
B	Q	H	S	O	M	L	I	L
T	R	A	H	K	D	A	T	K
M	O	O	S	E	E	F	F	C

VOWEL PLAY

1 Moth **2** Mosquito **3** Midge
4 Beetle **5** Locust **6** Termite
7 Gnat **8** Cicada **9** Earwig
10 Aphid

WORKOUT 58

SMART SUMS

1 36 (4x9) **2** 33 (26+7)
3 30 (90÷3) **4** 11 (5+6) **5** 6 (8-2)

MIND THE GAP

1 Ace **2** Lot **3** Pin **4** One
5 The

KAKURO

3	1		4	1	6	2		
1	2	5	9	3	8	6	4	7
	1	7	2	9			8	9

WORKOUT 59

ARROWORD

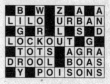

B		W		Z		A		A
L	I	L	O		U	R	B	A	N
	G		R		L		S		D
L	O	C	K	O	U	T		G
	T	O	T	S		A	G	R	A
D	R	O	O	L		B	O	A	S
	Y		P	O	I	S	O	N	S

FUTOSHIKI

2	3	1
1	2	3
3	1	2

SMALL CHANGE

1 Slipper, Sandal, Clog, Mule, Boot **2** Axe, Drill, Hammer, Saw, Clamp **3** Four, Fifty, Nine, One, Eight **4** Judge, Chef, Vet, Pilot, Cleaner **5** Rain, Shower, Snow, Hail, Sleet

WORKOUT 60

NUMBER JIG

1 383 **2** 927 **3** 7352 **4** 4461

CODEWORDS

1 Hen **2** Hare **3** Otter (9=T)
4 Stoat **5** Hornet

FOUR BY FOUR

F	U	N	K
A	R	E	A
I	D	O	L
R	U	N	E

SOLUTIONS

WORKOUT 61
IN AND OUT
Sort (- P), cheat (+ E), chart (+ R), them (- R), eyrie (+ Y) **PERRY** Camp (+ M), whet (- A), roué (- S), course (+ O), chat (- N) **MASON**

FOUR BY FOUR
B	A	L	E
E	X	I	T
A	L	E	C
M	E	S	H

SPLITS
1 Clingfilm 2 Interview
3 Furniture 4 Hairspray
5 Turquoise

WORKOUT 62
MINI JIGSAW
Cyprus, Poland, Turkey
Norway, France, Canada

KILLER SUDOKU
2	9	6	5	7	3	1	4	8
1	5	4	9	8	6	7	2	3
8	3	7	1	2	4	9	6	5
6	1	8	4	3	9	5	7	2
3	7	9	2	1	5	6	8	4
5	4	2	7	6	8	3	9	1
4	6	1	3	9	2	8	5	7
9	2	3	8	5	7	4	1	6
7	8	5	6	4	1	2	3	9

WORKOUT 63
INITIALS
1 Hundreds and thousands
2 *Keeping Up Appearances*
3 *Are You Lonesome Tonight?*
4 *Raiders of the Lost Ark*
5 Bull in a china shop

MISSING LINK
1 Wave 2 Nail 3 Mark
4 High 5 Foot. The constellation is VIRGO

FIX SIX

WORKOUT 64
WILD WORDS
1 You're under arrest 2 Forever
3 Cash in hand 4 No-one

ELIMINATION
Gemstones – Amber, Diamond, Jade, Jet, Opal.
DRAW – Attract, Pull, Raffle, Sketch, Tie.
BREAD – Crumb, Line, Sauce, Stick, Winner.
Parts of the face – Brow, Cheek, Chin, Lip, Nose.
Leftover phrase: BRASS BAND

COPYCATS
1 Wrong 2 Elver 3 Upright
4 4297 (4th, 1st, 3rd and 2nd digits) 5 Milk

WORKOUT 65
WORDSEARCH

VOWEL PLAY
1 Silk 2 Denim 3 Wool 4 Rayon
5 Tweed 6 Paisley 7 Plaid
8 Linen 9 Angora 10 Suede

CELL BLOCKS
	3		1		2
2	5				
			8		
3				4	
		3			3
				2	

WORKOUT 66
SUDOKU
1	4	3	2
2	3	4	1
4	1	2	3
3	2	1	4

1	2	4	3
3	4	1	2
2	1	3	4
4	3	2	1

1	4	2	3
2	3	1	4
4	1	3	2
3	2	4	1

ADD UP
1 37
2 35
3 46

WORKOUT 67
CODEWORD

SPOT THE SUM
1 22 (15+7) 2 29 (18+11)
3 30 (18+12) 4 35 (29+6)

WORKOUT 68
SCRAMBLE
1 Peru 2 Wales
3 Poland 4 Germany
5 Algeria 6 Thailand
7 Barbados 8 Cameroon

TENNIS MATCH
Photograph 4

WORKOUT 69

FUTOSHIKI

1	2	4	3
4	1	3	2
3	4	2	1
2	3	1	4

LETTER SEQUENCE

1 M (+3) **2** P (-2) **3** T
(-5, -4, -3...) **4** O (alternate
-1, +1) **5** J (January,
February...)

DISAVOWEL

R	A	D	I	S	H		H	O	C	K
A	R	O	M	A			B	A	R	O	N
S	I	M	P	L	E			P	A	R	E
P	E	E	L	E	D		P	L	E	A
	S		Y		I	C	E			D
D		J		A	T	O	N	E		
O	K	A	P	I		O	S	I	E	R
C	I	C	A	D	A			T		U
I	N	K	S		L	E	T	H	A	L
L	E	A	T	H	E	R		E	W	E
E		L			E	A	R	L	S	

WORKOUT 70

FITWORD

	S	O	U	R		O	P	S	
H		U		E		R		I	
E	A	T		V	Y	I	N	G	
A				E		G		H	
P	E	C	U	L	I	A	R		
S		I				M		A	
	F	R	E	T	T	I	N	G	
A		C		R			A		
B	U	L	G	E		C	H	I	
U		E		A		O		N	
T	O	D		D	E	B	T		

Rig

SET SQUARE

9	+	6	÷	3
−				+
2	×	5	−	1
+		−		×
7	+	8	−	4

WORKOUT 71

PATHFINDER

E	A	E	G	G	E	R	Y	D	E	R
S	G	L	O	D	E	W	G	A	L	C
S	O	R	L	F	B	I	R	D	F	U
O	U	D	R	A	U	O	R	I	E	P
R	G	O	R	Z	N	R	E	K	A	C
T	H	F	E	A	D	E	N	D	D	
A	B	L	A	H	F	A	O	U	B	Y
D	O	O	W	Y	A	I	H	G	I	T
G	E	L	L	A	W	R	N	C	P	
R	R	B	M	B	H	A	W	S	H	P
E	E	N	U	A	G	N	D	I	C	A

WOOD, GREEN, UMBRELLA, BAG,
HANDICAP, PITCH, SWING, HOLE,
ROUND, FAIRWAY, HAZARD,
ROUGH, FORE, ALBATROSS,
EAGLE, GOLF, BIRDIE, FLAG,
WEDGE, RYDER CUP, CADDY,
BUNKER

PAIRS

Black market, Channel Four,
coffee break, day school,
driving licence, English
breakfast, French dressing,
Green Party, head start, spoon-
feed, tablecloth, trick cyclist

STAIRS and TIRED yield DIRE
STRAITS

WORKOUT 72

HONEYCOMB

1 Far off 2 Ransom 3 Starve
4 Intend 5 Stroll 6 Malice
7 Common 8 Coward 9 Noodle
10&11 Norman Lamont

SUDOKU

2	1	4	9	6	7	5	3	8
9	3	6	1	8	5	4	7	2
7	5	8	2	3	4	6	1	9
3	7	1	4	5	8	2	9	6
5	8	9	6	1	2	3	4	7
4	6	2	3	7	9	1	8	5
1	2	3	8	9	6	7	5	4
6	9	5	7	4	1	8	2	3
8	4	7	5	2	3	9	6	1

MOBILE CODE

1 Oak 2 Pine 3 Cedar 4 Birch
5 Willow 6 Acacia

WORKOUT 73

WORD BUILDER

Reign, Grime, Arena, Miner,
Anger, Grain, German,
Remain, Marina, Armani,
Margin, Mirage, Manager,
Earring, Marriage,
Margarine

WORDSEARCH

OPPOSITES ATTRACT

1 Sour/Sweet **2** Loose/Tight
3 Strong/Weak **4** Entrance/
Exit **5** Cheap/Expensive

WORKOUT 74

MEMORY QUIZ

1 Green **2** Seven **3** No,
it's supersede **4** The right
5 Green **6** V

SMART SUMS

1 4 (8-4) **2** 6 (30÷5) **3** 20
(4x5) **4** 54 (60-6) **5** 67 (64+3)

KAKURO

1	3		4	6	1	2	
2	1	5	9	8	3	6	4	7
		1	7	9	2		8	9

SOLUTIONS

WORKOUT 75
ARROWORD

STAIRCASE
Strauss, Mahler, Elgar, Britten, Dvorak, Rossini, Glinka.
The "staircase" reveals: SMETANA

SMALL CHANGE
1 Large, Big, Vast, Whopping, Massive **2** Helmet, Pump, Bike, Ride, Pedal **3** Ramble, March, Walk, Strut, Hike **4** Steam, Cook, Poach, Simmer, Fry

WORKOUT 76
NUMBER JIG
1 259 **2** 217 **3** 9464 **4** 3517

SPLITS
1 Partridge **2** Something **3** Quarterly **4** Carthorse **5** Bamboozle

FOUR BY FOUR

WORKOUT 77
NINERS
Chemistry, labyrinth, apartment, numerical
The left-hand column gives **CLAN**.

ALL FOURS

C	O	R	K
A	M	E	N
R	I	L	E
S	T	Y	E

BOX WISE
1 Cou **2** Rai **3** Sin **4** Ful **5** Lad **6** Led **7** Fil **8** Thy **9** Ger **10** Bil **11** Let **12** Low

WORKOUT 78
MINI JIGSAW
Monkey, Rabbit, Jaguar
Ferret, Donkey, Badger

KILLER SUDOKU

8	4	7	3	9	6	5	2	1
5	3	2	7	1	4	6	8	9
9	6	1	2	8	5	3	7	4
4	2	6	9	3	8	1	5	7
1	9	5	4	7	2	8	3	6
3	7	8	6	5	1	9	4	2
7	1	4	5	6	3	2	9	8
2	8	3	1	4	9	7	6	5
6	5	9	8	2	7	4	1	3

WORKOUT 79
FUTOSHIKI

3	1	2
1	2	3
2	3	1

3	2	1
2	1	3
1	3	2

2	3	1
1	2	3
3	1	2

WORD BUILDER
Apron, Prong, Groan, Spine, Orange, Ignore, Senior, Pigeon, Parson, Rope in, Sponger, Open-air, Iron Age, Searing, Organise, Singapore

WORKOUT 80
FARE'S FAIR

	R	A	Y	S
P	A	N	E	
S	I	D	E	
C	O	U	R	T
	D	E	W	
S	A	W		

SPLITS
1 Underwear **2** Evergreen **3** Community **4** Athletics **5** Miniature

WORKOUT 81
LOGICAL
Tom, Lake District, Chocolate
Dick, Peak District, Tea bags
Harry, Yorkshire Dales, Brandy

CELL BLOCKS

WORKOUT 82
SUDOKU

4	3	1	2
1	2	4	3
2	4	3	1
3	1	2	4

1	3	4	2
4	2	1	3
2	1	3	4
3	4	2	1

2	3	4	1
4	1	3	2
1	4	2	3
3	2	1	4

WORDSEARCH

WORKOUT 83
CODEWORD

SO COMPLETE

Wild,	wide,	idle	D
Warn,	wren,	wear	R
Dear,	moat,	alas	A
Café,	ford,	leaf	F
Test,	mate,	sett	T

WORKOUT 84
SPOT THE SUM

1 21 (14+7) **3** 36 (32+4)
2 24 (15+9) **4** 33 (28+5)

PIECEWORD

WORKOUT 85
SCRAMBLE

1 Comet **2** Evans
3 Burton **4** Virgin **5** Iceland
6 Top Shop **7** Mothercare
8 Waterstones

FOUR BY FOUR

L	A	U	D
A	W	R	Y
C	A	G	E
E	Y	E	D

TOWN TO TOWN
HARLECH

1 Rachel **2** Clear **3** Real
4 Era **5** Mare **6** Amber
7 Beamer **BRAEMAR**

WORKOUT 86
FITWORD

Vagabond

SIX PACK

WORKOUT 87
PATHFINDER

THE BOYFRIEND, CHICAGO,
MAME, INTO THE WOODS, FUNNY
FACE, MAMMA MIA, GREASE,
SWEET CHARITY, THE LION KING,
MARY POPPINS, BRIGADOON,
GODSPELL, OKLAHOMA, HAIR

SOUNDALIKES

1 Knew/new **2** Stile/style
3 I'll/aisle **4** Mussels/muscles

COPYCATS

1 Duck **2** 169 (square numbers)
3 Dame (replace 3rd letter with
next one in the alphabet) **4** Bow

WORKOUT 88
BUZZ OFF

1 and 6

SUDOKU

9	4	8	2	6	1	3	5	7
2	1	5	8	7	3	4	9	6
7	6	3	4	5	9	8	2	1
6	3	2	5	8	4	7	1	9
4	7	1	9	2	6	5	8	3
8	5	9	3	1	7	6	4	2
5	8	6	7	9	2	1	3	4
3	2	7	1	4	5	9	6	8
1	9	4	6	3	8	2	7	5

SPLITS

1 Concerned **2** Machinist
3 Beautiful **4** Boulevard
5 Pageantry

WORKOUT 89
DOMINOES

1 Ashley **2** Mickey
3 Imelda **4** Dougal
5 Gareth **6** Nasser

WORDSEARCH

FUTOSHIKI

1	3	2
2	1	3
3	2	1

WORKOUT 90
SMART SUMS

1 36 (4+32) **2** 1396
(1488-92) **3** 52 (20+32)
4 48 (3x16) **5** 33 (51-18)

SMALL CHANGE

1 Snap, Bridge, Rummy,
Poker, Whist **2** Fairy, Imp,
Troll, Elf, Peri **3** Bake,
Roast, Grill, Stew, Poach
4 Deacon, Dean, Verger,
Beadle, Pastor

KAKURO

3	1		4	6	1	2		
1	2	5	9	8	3	6	4	7
		1	7	9	2		8	9

SOLUTIONS

WORKOUT 91
ARROWORD

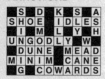

VOWEL PLAY
1 Judo 2 Polo 3 Aerobics
4 Karate 5 Boxing 6 Diving
7 Rugby 8 Tennis 9 Archery
10 Football

TWO OF A KIND
1 Convent/nunnery
2 Consider/deliberate
3 Result/upshot 4 Fuming/
ireful 5 Giggling/laughter

WORKOUT 92
FIX SIX

MOBILE CODE
1 Derby 2 Truro 3 Exeter
4 Ipswich 5 Taunton

INITIALS
1 The Virgin Queen 2 *To Kill a Mockingbird* 3 *The Winner Takes it All* 4 *Kind Hearts and Coronets* 5 Neither a borrower nor a lender be

WORKOUT 93
MIND THE GAP
Despair, Alarmed, Gnasher, Steamer, Enforce, Educate, Timpani, Haulier.

The shaded word is:
PASTRAMI

FOUR BY FOUR

BOX WISE
1 Mar 2 Pur 3 Lin 4 Ger
5 Gey 6 Ser 7 Bil 8 Low
9 Ver 10 Bal 11 Let 12 Sam

WORKOUT 94
MINI JIGSAW
Boxing, Shinty, Tennis
Squash, Hockey, Skiing

KILLER SUDOKU

6	2	7	3	5	8	4	1	9
8	1	3	4	9	2	7	6	5
9	4	5	7	1	6	3	8	2
1	6	9	5	7	3	8	2	4
3	7	8	2	4	1	5	9	6
4	5	2	6	8	9	1	7	3
2	8	1	9	3	5	6	4	7
5	9	4	1	6	7	2	3	8
7	3	6	8	2	4	9	5	1

WORKOUT 95
WORD BUILDER
Peace, Nacre, Erect, Caper, Pecan, Crate, Recent, Career, Carpet, Create, Centre, Nectar, Terrace, Reenact, Retrace, Carpenter

NUMBER JIG
1 897 2 435 3 5768 4 1212

WORKOUT 96
IN AND OUT
Steam (+ T), cream (+ E), tough (- R), Spain (- R), tansy (+ Y) **TERRY**

Town (+ W), tut (- A), ideal (+ I), sleigh (- T), crate (- E) **WAITE**

SET SQUARE

9	+	6	÷	3
+		×		×
1	+	4	÷	5
×		−		−
2	×	7	−	8

ELIMINATION
KEY – Board, Note, Pad, Ring, Stone.
Space – Moon, Orbit, Planet, Satellite, Star.
Pastry – Choux, Filo, Flaky, Puff, Shortcrust.
LU lines – Bakerloo, Central, Circle, Jubilee, Northern.

Leftover word: **WHOLEMEAL**

WORKOUT 97
WORDSEARCH

SPLITS
1 Miserable 2 Hysterics
3 Parachute 4 Essential
5 Starboard

CELL BLOCKS

WORKOUT 98

SUDOKU

4	1	2	3
3	2	4	1
1	4	3	2
2	3	1	4

2	4	1	3
1	3	2	4
3	2	4	1
4	1	3	2

3	2	4	1
4	1	3	2
2	4	1	3
1	3	2	4

ADD UP

1 44
2 48
3 36

SCRAMBLE

1 Cape 2 Dale 3 West
4 Shore 5 Desert 6 Stream
7 Coppice 8 Estuary
9 Snowcap 10 Everglades

PYRAMID

1 A 2 Ta 3 Sat 4 Tans
5 Saint 6 Tisane 7 Estonia
8 Obeisant 9 Baritones

WORKOUT 102

FITWORD

H	A	V	O	C		B	U	Y
E		O		L		A		E
R	A	W		O	N	S	E	T
E				W		M		I
B	I	A	N	N	U	A	L	
Y		R				T		A
	S	T	A	F	F	I	N	G
I		W	U					E
D	R	O	S	S		K	I	N
E		R	E		O			C
A	S	K		D	A	I	L	Y

Gargle

ALPHA-BEATER

C	F		F	E	Z		J	
H	E	A	V	E		A	L	L	O	T
I		B		L		P		K
C	A	L	L	O	W		I	C	E	D
	E		N		Q		I	
M	O	D	E		J	U	T	T	E	D
N		G		A		R		A
H	Y	E	N	A		R	O	U	S	T
X			P	E	T		S		E

WORKOUT 103

PATHFINDER

ANEMONE, NERINE, TULIP, SNOWDROP,
GLADIOLUS, IXIA, BEGONIA, DAFFODIL,
DAHLIA, LILY, BLUEBELL, ALLIUM,
ACONITE, SCILLA, CROCUS, JONQUIL,
FREESIA, MONTBRETIA

WORKOUT 99

CODEWORD

D	D		B	S	J		T
G	A	Z	E	B	O		H	E	E	D	E	D
Y		W		N		R		T
S	T	A	Y		S	K	I	T	T	I	S	H
I		L		A		L		I
I	M	P	E	R	I	A	L	I	S	M
E		A		O		G		I
	P	R	O	V	I	D	E	N	T	L	Y
S		P		O		E		U
S	Q	U	I	R	R	E	L		F	A	C	T
U		E		T		V		A		O
G	A	U	C	H	E		E	X	C	E	S	S
D		E		X		D		E		E

COPYCATS

1 0.4 2 Crave 3 Virtue
4 Pearl 5 Tray

WORKOUT 100

SHAPE UP

C	P	E	B	H	E	B	N	P	F
A	O	U	A	A	P	A	E	U	U
M	P	S	L	R	P	R	W	T	L
D	L	T	H	R	I	N	H	N	H
E	A	O	A	O	N	E	A	E	A
N	R	N	M	W	G	T	M	Y	M

WORKOUT 101

CODEWORDS

1 Tea 2 Wine 3 Cider
4 Soda 5 Retsina

FUTOSHIKI

3	1	2
2	3	1
1	2	3

SMALL CHANGE

1 Ferry, Tug, Junk,
Canoe, Tanker 2 Dupe,
Trick, Con, Cheat, Gull
3 Snow, Frost, Hail, Rain,
Sleet 4 Prawn, Crab,
Clam, Winkle, Cockle

WORKOUT 104

DISAVOWEL

O	B	O	E		P	L	U	R	A	L
R	O	U	E		A		N	O	V	A
A	S	T	R	A	L		D	A	I	S
L	U	R	I	D		H	O	R	D	E
	N	E	E	D		O		I		R
E		A		T	W	I	N	E	
R	O	C	O	C	O		O	G	R	E
A	S	H	L	A	R		N		E
	I		D	R	I	E	S	T		B
R	E	N	E	G	E		O	V	A	
	R		R	O	S	A	R	Y		A

SUDOKU

1	9	7	8	3	2	4	6	5
8	3	4	7	6	5	2	1	9
5	6	2	4	9	1	7	3	8
6	8	5	2	1	3	9	4	7
4	2	3	9	5	7	6	8	1
9	7	1	6	4	8	3	5	2
2	4	9	5	8	6	1	7	3
3	5	6	1	7	9	8	2	4
7	1	8	3	2	4	5	9	6

THREE IN ONE

1 Bill 2 Chair 3 Common
4 Wear 5 Spell

SOLUTIONS

WORKOUT 105

MINI FIT
1 Tut 2 Flu 3 Ally 4 Corn

WORDSEARCH

CODEWORD
1 Sea 2 Crab 3 Coast (9=T)
4 Resort 5 Bathers

WORKOUT 106

MIND THE GAP
1 Tin 2 Par 3 Hat 4 The 5 Pat

MEMORY QUIZ
1 Eagle 2 Portcullis
3 *EastEnders* 4 Blue
5 Morecambe 6 Red

KAKURO

WORKOUT 107

ARROWORD

VOWEL PLAY
1 Pug 2 Boxer 3 Corgi 4 Beagle
5 Collie 6 Lurcher 7 Samoyed
8 Alsatian 9 Retriever 10 Terrier

CODEWORDS
1 Mike 2 Lima 3 Echo
4 Sierra 5 Charlie

WORKOUT 108

WORDSEARCH

LETTER SEQUENCE
1 T (+2, +4, +3, repeated)
2 F (+13, -11, +13, -10,
+13, -9 etc) 3 T (alternate
in pairs +1, +2; +1, +3; +1,
+4 etc) 4 V (initial letters of
rainbow colours) 5 E (initials
of British monarchs from
George IV onwards). Well
done if you got 4 and 5

FOUR BY FOUR

WORKOUT 109

PAIRS
Backgammon, beanpole,
birthstone, doormat,
front-runner, market day,
mountain bike, penny black,
Royal Marine, string vest,
table manners, visiting card
Safe recipe – Fire escape

SPLITS
1 Barricade 2 Enunciate
3 Ingenious 4 Featuring
5 Hideously

BOX WISE
1 But 2 Car 3 Ton 4 Ing
5 Par 6 Rot 7 Est 8 Eem
9 Ten 10 Don 11 Ate 12 Key

WORKOUT 110

MINI JIGSAW
Blazer, Kimono, Blouse
Jersey, Shorts, Anorak

SO COMPLETE
Draw,   dawn,   swan   W
White,   ashen,   hoist   H
Pain,   shift,   like   I
Morass, caress, chase   S
King,   wink,   skin   K

WORKOUT 111

WORD BUILDER
Pslam, Prams, Slump, Prism,
Maria, Mails, Plums, Murals,
Plasma, Salami, Primal,
Alarms, Samurai, Impalas,
Marsupial

TAKE FIVE

E	I	G	H	T
I		A		A
G	A	V	E	L
H		E		O
T	A	L	O	N

WORKOUT 112

WILD WORDS
1 Lion King 2 Six of one,
half-a-dozen of the other
3 Crossroads 4 Caught in
the act

MISSING LINK
1 Cold 2 Knee 3 Time
4 Book 5 Land – Lemon

ELIMINATION
Body parts – Café (face),
Earth (heart), Viler (liver),
Keen (knee), Lose (sole)

Green things – Emerald,
Grass, Jade, Lime, Olive

OIL – Drum, Rig, Slick, Skin,
Well

Square numbers – Four, Nine,
One, Sixteen, Twenty-five

Leftover word: **TWO-STEP**

WORKOUT 113

MINI FIT
1 Ode 2 Pat

CELL BLOCKS

WORKOUT 114

SUDOKU

3	1	4	2
2	4	3	1
1	3	2	4
4	2	1	3

3	2	1	4
1	4	2	3
2	3	4	1
4	1	3	2

2	4	3	1
3	1	2	4
4	3	1	2
1	2	4	3

ADD UP
1 50
2 39
3 60

WORKOUT 115

CODEWORD

SPOT THE SUM
1 23 (9+14) 2 20 (4+16)
3 18 (4+14) 4 32 (13+19)

WORKOUT 116

NINERS

Blackmail, replenish, automaton, yesterday
The left-hand column gives **BRAY**.

MANE LINE
Photograph 1

WORKOUT 117

MOBILE CODE
1 Cole 2 Clooney 3 Formby
4 Foreman 5 Michael 6 Peppard

LOGICAL

Curly, 5 years, football, West
Hambo, 3 years, truffle hunting, South
Trotter, 4 years, mudbath, North

HONEYCOMB

1 Thrice 2 Docile 3 Nursed
4 Almost 5 Oracle 6 Fleece
7 Confer 8 Grouse 9 Raisin
10&11 Second fiddle

WORKOUT 118

FITWORD

Dew

SET SQUARE

1	+	6	×	4
+		×		÷
7	+	9	÷	2
÷		÷		+
8	+	3	−	5

WORKOUT 119

PATHFINDER

MAORI, SWEDISH, HINDI, FRENCH, KASHMIRI, WELSH, ENGLISH, RUSSIAN, CZECH, URDU, JAPANESE, ROMANY, SWAHILI, TURKISH, ICELANDIC, POLISH, DUTCH, PUNJABI, SPANISH

NUMBER JIG
1 284 2 153 3 6621

ALPHA-FIT

WORKOUT 120

PYRAMID

1 E 2 Re 3 Ire 4 Erin
5 Miner 6 Remain 7 Minaret
8 Terminal 9 Tramlines

SUDOKU

4	5	7	3	6	8	9	1	2
6	2	8	5	9	1	7	4	3
1	3	9	2	4	7	6	8	5
9	7	5	4	8	2	3	6	1
8	1	6	9	5	3	2	7	4
3	4	2	1	7	6	8	5	9
7	9	4	8	2	5	1	3	6
2	8	1	6	3	4	5	9	7
5	6	3	7	1	9	4	2	8

STAIRCASE

Yellow, Darling, Danube, Ganges, Trent, Zambezi, Garonne. The "staircase" reveals: YANGTZE

SOLUTIONS

WORKOUT 121

SUDOKU

1	2	4	3
4	3	2	1
3	4	1	2
2	1	3	4

2	4	3	1
1	3	2	4
3	1	4	2
4	2	1	3

3	1	4	2
2	4	3	1
1	3	2	4
4	2	1	3

WORDSEARCH

FOUR BY FOUR

W	I	R	E
E	D	E	N
L	E	A	D
D	A	D	S

WORKOUT 122

SMART SUMS
1 2 (14÷7) **2** 10 (6+4) **3** 16 (4x4)
4 202 (204-2) **5** 72 (24x3)

OPPOSITES ATTRACT
1 Broke/loaded **2** Separate/together **3** Private/public
4 Correct/improper

KAKURO

		2	4	1	6		8	9
2	1	6	9	3	8	5	4	7
1	3		7	2	9	1		

WORKOUT 123

ARROWORD

SPLITS
1 Essayists **2** Fireproof
3 Scholarly **4** Runaround
5 Dexterity

LOGICAL
Sanjeev, Gold, Long jump
Chuck, Silver, 100m
Russell, Bronze, Discus

WORKOUT 124

CAKE BAKE
3 and 4

TWO OF A KIND
1 Absolute/complete
2 Magnate/tycoon
3 Enormity/vastness
4 Constant/permanent
5 Champion/victor

STAIRCASE
Cradle, Tallboy, Table,
Divan, Bench, Rocker,
Whatnot.

The furniture item is:

CABINET

WORKOUT 125

FARE'S FAIR

R	I	G	H	T
		T	I	M	E
	S	A	N	E
R	E	I	G	N
I	D	L	E
F	A	R	E

FUTOSHIKI

1	3	2

2	1	3

3	2	1

WORKOUT 126

MINI JIGSAW
Sorbet, Mousse, Trifle
Yogurt, Sundae, Gateau

KILLER SUDOKU

9	3	4	6	7	5	8	1	2
1	8	5	2	9	3	4	7	6
7	6	2	1	4	8	5	3	9
5	1	3	8	6	2	7	9	4
4	2	6	7	3	9	1	5	8
8	9	7	4	5	1	6	2	3
6	4	9	5	2	7	3	8	1
2	5	8	3	1	6	9	4	7
3	7	1	9	8	4	2	6	5

WORKOUT 127

WORD BUILDER
Antic, Dance, Acute, Enact,
Ocean, Tonic, Canoe,
Toucan, Action, Deacon,
Induce, Octane, Noticed,
Counted, Conduit, Cautioned,
Auctioned, Education

WORDSEARCH

WORKOUT 128

NINERS
Recollect, orphanage, mincemeat, eastwards
The left-hand column gives **ROME**.

SET SQUARE

7	×	8	÷	4
+		−		+
9	+	1	−	5
−		×		÷
6	×	2	−	3

ELIMINATION
Reindeer – Comet, Cupid, Dasher, Dancer, Vixen.
___ Ball – Hand, Odd, Pin, Punch, Screw.
Egg-layers – Bee, Goose, Platypus, Salmon, Turtle.
Dances – Foxtrot, Jive, Samba, Tango, Waltz.

Leftover phrase:
PRINCIPAL BOY

WORKOUT 129

WORDSEARCH

PAIRS
Armrest, borderline, bow tie, breakneck, chairwoman, cricket pitch, downmarket, French window, garden centre, outfield, scarlet fever, spread eagle

GERM and VALIANT yield MALT VINEGAR

CELL BLOCKS

WORKOUT 130

SUDOKU

1	4	3	2
3	2	4	1
4	1	2	3
2	3	1	4

4	1	3	2
3	2	1	4
1	4	2	3
2	3	4	1

4	2	1	3
1	3	4	2
2	1	3	4
3	4	2	1

ADD UP
1 36
2 48
3 31

WORKOUT 131

CODEWORD

1 Green 2 Left 3 Broccoli
4 Left 5 £5 note – the Queen and Elizabeth Fry 6 Red

WORKOUT 132

SPLITS
1 Periphery 2 Childcare
3 Mutineers 4 Menagerie
5 Weathered

BABY FACE
Photograph 3

WORKOUT 133

NUMBER SEQUENCE
1 91 (+(2x2), +(3x3) etc)
2 30 (+8,-2,+9,-3, +10,-4 etc) **3** 6 (this one's tricky – it's the number of letters in the names of the months, starting with January)
4 58 (sum of the numbers 1 and 3 places before)
5 70 (+(2x2),+(2x2x2) etc)

INITIALS
1 King Kong **2** *Oranges and Lemons* **3** The Lake District **4** The Leaning Tower of Pisa **5** *Joseph and the Amazing Technicolour Dreamcoat*

PYRAMID
1 E **2** Te **3** Set **4** Rest
5 Steer **6** Teaser **7** Serrate
8 Traverse **9** Harvester

WORKOUT 134

FITWORD

C	O	C	O	A		B	U	T
A		R		L		A		A
T	E	A		S	I	D	E	S
T		M		O				T
Y	I	P	S		S	T	A	Y
		E						
R	O	D	E		S	N	O	B
O			R		T			A
G	U	S	T	O		I	T	S
U		O		O				I
E	B	B		M	O	G	U	L

Farce

WORD BUILDER
Alien, Agent, Navel, Angel, Naïve, Angle, Native, Ignite, Genial, Invite, Tangle, Entail, Leaving, Vintage, Tailing, Veiling, Vigilant, Valeting, Vigilante

SOLUTIONS

WORKOUT 135
PATHFINDER

FARFALLE, FUSILLI, MACARONI, NOODLES, LASAGNE, RADIATORE, RIGATONI, TAGLIATELLE, CONCHIGLIE, LINGUINE, PASTA, SPAGHETTI, VERMICELLI, GEMELLI, RAVIOLI

NUMBER JIG
1 121 **2** 942 **3** 3689

LEAF ALONE

WORKOUT 136
SPOT THE SUM
1 22 (15+7) **2** 29 (18+11) **3** 30 (18+12) **4** 35 (29+6)

SUDOKU

1	8	5	6	2	7	4	3	9
4	7	9	3	8	5	1	6	2
3	2	6	4	1	9	7	8	5
7	3	2	9	5	1	6	4	8
5	9	1	8	4	6	3	2	7
6	4	8	2	7	3	9	5	1
9	5	4	7	6	2	8	1	3
8	1	7	5	3	4	2	9	6
2	6	3	1	9	8	5	7	4

SCRAMBLE
1 Leo **2** Aries **3** Orion **4** Plough **5** Pisces **6** Great bear **7** Andromeda **8** Capricorn

WORKOUT 137
SIX PACK

WORD SEARCH

SMART SUMS
1 32 (144-112) **2** 150 (366-216) **3** 48 (4x12) **4** 27 (6+21) **5** 81 (9x9)

WORKOUT 138
COPYCATS
1 Clarinet **2** Gape (1st and 3rd letter pattern: 1 lower and 2 lower) **3** Cricket **4** Asia **5** Gas

KAKURO

	9	7		1	3		1	3
7	8	9	6	5	1	3	2	4
9	5		7	9		1	5	

WORKOUT 139
ARROWORD

		N		I		G		A
S	C	R	I	P	T	U	R	E	S
	R		G		V	O		K
B	A	T	H	S		C	U	T
N	O	T	E	P	A	P	E	R
B	E	G	I	N		S	I	L	O
	S	E	D	A	T	E	L	Y

VOWEL PLAY
1 Bay **2** Mace **3** Mint **4** Sage **5** Anise **6** Borage **7** Aniseed **8** Oregano **9** Rosemary **10** Turmeric

SMALL CHANGE
1 Hall, Loft, Chamber, Suite, Cellar **2** Bloom, Stalk, Petal, Leaf, Seed **3** Sole, Tyne, Dogger, Dover, Bailey **4** Hearing, Touch, Sight, Taste, Smell **5** Joy, Bliss, Glee, Rapture, Exultation

WORKOUT 140
FIX SIX

MOBILE CODE
1 Sum **2** Mean **3** Root **4** Value **5** Matrix

FOUR BY FOUR

B	O	O	K
A	C	M	E
W	H	E	Y
L	E	N	S

WORKOUT 141
SET SQUARE

8	−	4	×	9
−		×		÷
1	×	6	÷	3
×		÷		+
5	×	2	−	7

TAKE FIVE

T	A	B	L	E
A		R		B
B	R	A	V	O
L		V		N
E	B	O	N	Y

MIND THE GAP
Secured, Deviant, Deplete, Trouser, Spangle, Maidens, Hoaxers, Reproof.

The shaded word is: **CALENDAR**

SOLUTIONS

WORKOUT 142

MINI JIGSAW
Carafe, Scales, Cooker, Fridge, Juicer, Larder

KILLER SUDOKU

9	1	5	7	2	3	6	4	8
8	2	4	6	1	5	9	3	7
6	3	7	9	4	8	1	2	5
5	4	8	3	6	9	2	7	1
7	9	2	4	5	1	8	6	3
1	6	3	8	7	2	5	9	4
3	5	6	1	9	4	7	8	2
4	7	1	2	8	6	3	5	9
2	8	9	5	3	7	4	1	6

WORKOUT 143

MINI FIT
1 Awn **2** Lap **3** Wash **4** Apse

DOMINOES
1 Paella **2** Lychee **3** Cashew
4 Cassis **5** Raisin **6** Panini

WORKOUT 144

STEP RIDDLE
Limes, Times, Tomes, Tones, Tongs, Tonga

BOX WISE
1 Sto **2** War **3** Red **4** Der
5 Gar **6** Den **7** Mal **8** Let
9 Tal **10** Ent **11** Ice **12** Rap

SOUNDALIKES
1 Ruff/rough **2** Main/mein
3 Brewed/brood **4** Whine/wine

WORKOUT 145

WORDSEARCH

SPL...ter 2 Porcelain
1 ...ander 4 Geography
Manifesto

CELL BLOCKS

		3			3
	3			2	
3			3		
	4			2	
3					
	3		3		4

WORKOUT 146

SUDOKU

4	3	1	2
1	2	4	3
3	1	2	4
2	4	3	1

4	3	2	1
2	1	4	3
3	2	1	4
1	4	3	2

3	4	1	2
1	2	4	3
4	3	2	1
2	1	3	4

ADD UP
1 31 **2** 36 **3** 41

WORKOUT 147

CODEWORD

THREE IN ONE
1 Case **2** Pen **3** Last **4** Jet
5 Hold

WORKOUT 148

SHAPE UP

L	B	B	T	G	T	B	F	S	B
O	O	R	U	A	R	O	E	A	O
A	A	O	R	L	I	O	D	N	W
F	T	G	B	O	L	T	O	D	L
E	E	U	A	S	B	E	R	A	E
R	R	E	N	H	Y	E	A	L	R

WORKOUT 149

FUTOSHIKI

1	3	4	2
2	1	3	4
4	2	1	3
3	4	2	1

CODEWORDS
1 Pea **2** Corn **3** Caper
4 Crisp **5** Scone

TOWN TO TOWN
DALSTON
1 Talons **2** Altos **3** Last
4 Sat **5** Teas **6** Hates
7 Thames
WEST HAM

WORKOUT 150

FITWORD

L	U	R	K		G	A	R	B
O		O			O		O	
B		S	E	E	C	H	E	D
		T		M		E		Y
T	I	P	P	I	N	G		
U			E		I		E	
T	E	A	R	I	N	G		
A		X		O		O		F
S	U	P	E	R	S	T	A	R
		A		A				A
I	O	T	A		I	D	L	Y

Sarcastic

SPOT THE SUM
1 33 (14+19) **2** 33 (12+21)
3 21 (3+18) **4** 34 (6+28)

SOLUTIONS

WORKOUT 151
PATHFINDER

SUSPECT, REVEREND GREEN, LIBRARY, REVOLVER, SPANNER, HALL, BALLROOM, PROFESSOR PLUM, ROPE, WHODUNNIT, DAGGER, LEAD PIPING, DINING ROOM, WEAPON, STUDY, CARD

ADD UP
1 26 **2** 60 **3** 42

IN AND OUT
Dance (+ C), nice (- H), glean (+ A), claim (+ I), vie (- N) **CHAIN**

Roué (- S), pleat (+ T), shut (- O), spires (+ R), wave (- E) **STORE**

FOUR BY FOUR

C	O	W	S
A	B	E	T
S	O	L	E
H	E	L	P

KAKURO

WORKOUT 153
WORD BUILDER
Feast, Feats, Cafes, Feint, Facts, Faint, Fiesta, Fasten, Finest, Fiance, Infest, Facets, Fanciest, Fanatics, Fascinate

WORDSEARCH

SPLITS
1 Demanding **2** Infringes
3 Digestive **4** Secretary
5 Crimplene

WORKOUT 155
ARROWORD

INITIALS
1 *All Creatures Great and Small* **2** Pickled onion
3 Sherlock Holmes and Dr Watson **4** *My Heart Will Go On* **5** All's Well That Ends Well

VOWEL PLAY
1 Noel **2** Carol **3** Reindeer
4 Bauble **5** Tree **6** Grotto
7 Elf **8** Santa **9** Wreath
10 Wenceslas

WORKOUT 152
COMPLETE WORKS
Rich	sham	bash
Shear	laver	amber
Drive	alive	aven
Strop	Stout	choir
Price	Click	cheat

H A V O

SUDOKU

WORKOUT 154
SUDOKU

WILDWORDS
1 Jagged edge
2 I understand
3 Backbone
4 Rising damp
5 Round of applause

WORKOUT 156
ODD ONE OUT
Picture 4

SCRAMBLE
1 Etna **2** Sinai **3** Snowdon
4 Everest **5** McKinley
6 ...rhorn **7** Krakatoa
...aro

FOUR...

B	O	W	S
O	V	A	L
M	E	R	E
B	R	E	D

18

SOLUTIONS

WORKOUT 157

HONEYCOMB
1 Annual 2 Finale 3 Morsel
4 Almond 5 Kaolin 6 Wicket
7 Kitten 8 Attend 9 Tureen
10 & 11 Tennis racket

MIND THE GAP
1 Win 2 Arc 3 Sew 4 Get 5 Nab

MISSING LINK
1 Pace 2 Walk 3 Slow
4 Sour 5 Tide. The weather
feature is: **CLOUD**

WORKOUT 158

MINI JIGSAW
Palace, Church, Prison
Museum, Hostel, Garage

KILLER SUDOKU

5	4	7	8	6	1	2	9	3
6	1	2	3	9	4	7	8	5
9	8	3	5	2	7	6	1	4
2	5	8	4	1	9	3	7	6
3	6	1	2	7	8	4	5	9
7	9	4	6	5	3	1	2	8
1	7	6	9	4	5	8	3	2
4	3	9	1	8	2	5	6	7
8	2	5	7	3	6	9	4	1

WORKOUT 159

NUMBER JIG

7		8	1	4	9	5		4
9	1	4	2		3	5	1	6
1	2	2	0		5	5	2	2
3	3	3		1	3	5	3	1
	9		1	4	9		6	
1	8	5	3	1		1	7	4
7	7	5		2	1	8	3	
7	6	9	8		5	6	9	8
1		6	1	2	9	3		0

Leftover number: **4523**

MINI FIT
1 Tin 2 Dog 3 Road 4 Claw

WORKOUT 160

ELIMINATION
Adverbs – Fast, Greedily,
Happily, Much, Well.

Young animals – Calf, Chick,
Kid, Lamb, Puppy.

Hats – Bowler, Cloche,
Mitre, Topper, Trilby.

SLEEP synonyms – Doze,
Kip, Nap, Slumber, Snooze.

Remaining: **HOTHEAD**

FARE'S FAIR

```
  S H O R E
  L Y N X
    P H L O X
R I G H T
    S E E N
  B A N D
```

SET SQUARE

8	+	3	×	2
÷		+		×
4	+	9	−	5
×		÷		−
7	+	6	−	1

WORKOUT 161

WORDSEARCH

COPYCATS
1 Link (reverse word and
add K) 2 7 (9 lower) 3 Sting
(weapon) 4 Mast (first letter
eight higher in the alphabet)
5 Breed (second vowel one
vowel higher)

CELL BLOCKS

			4	
5			4	4
	3	2		
		1		2
			5	
3			3	

WORKOUT 162

SUDOKU

3	2	1	4
1	4	3	2
2	1	4	3
4	3	2	1

4	1	2	3
2	3	4	1
1	2	3	4
3	4	1	2

4	3	2	1
2	1	3	4
3	4	1	2
1	2	4	3

ADD UP
1 30
2 33
3 46

WORKOUT 163

CODEWORDS

```
U N F L A T T E R I N G
A   A   A   E   J   M   R
S E I Z U R E   E L A T E
S   V   D   T   C   G   W
A X E D   W E A T H E R
U   L   T   R   I       G
L A Y M A N   M O H A I R
T   X   F   N   Q   E
  S T A P L E R   Q U I N
K   A   A   E   V   A   A
I T C H Y   B L A S T E D
W   I   E   L   N   I   E
I N T E R F E R E N C E
```

SPOT THE SUM
1 23 (9+14) 2 20 (4+16)
3 18 (4+14) 4 32 (13+19)

219

SOLUTIONS

WORKOUT 164
PIECEWORD

	G		W		C	R	I	S	I	S
C	A	R	R	O	T		E		O	C
	T		O		R	E	P	U	L	S	E
H	E	R	N	I	A		E		V	N
A		G		W	I	L	D	E	S	T
C	U	P	F	U	L		A		A	
A		U			T	U	R	N	E	D
P	A	R	L	O	U	R		I		A
A		A		W		I	G	N	O	R	E
B	O	T	A	N	I	C		G		W
L		E		E		E	C	L	A	I	R
E	N	D	U	R	E			Y		G

WORKOUT 165
FUTOSHIKI

2	3	1
1	2	3
3	1	2

SPLITS

1 Meringues 2 Historian
3 Rigmarole 4 Leniently
5 Patriarch

DISAVOWEL

O	R	A	L		J		P	O	O	L
R	E	C	I	T	A	L		R	U	E
G	A	T	E	A	U		C	A	R	S
A	D	O		U	N	C	U	T		I
N		R	A	N	D		P	O	L	O
	B		S	T	I	R		R	U	N
R	O	M	P		C	O	N		P	
H	O	E		M	E	L	O	D	I	C
I	N	D	I	A		L	I	A	N	A
N		I		G	U	E	S	T		L
O	K	A	P	I		R	E	A	L	M

WORKOUT 166
FITWORD

	G	U	L	L	I	B	L	E
A		S		I		A		I
C	H	E	C	K		T	U	G
I			E	A	T		H	
D	A	T	E	D		L	O	T
	O				E			E
C	U	R		V	I	R	U	S
H		R	O	E				A
I	R	E		N	E	W	L	Y
N		N	O		A			A
O	P	T	I	M	I	S	T	

Zest

SHAPE UP

D	T	M	D	B	W	H	C	B	W
E	A	A	V	A	A	A	H	R	E
L	L	H	O	R	G	N	O	A	B
I	L	L	R	T	N	D	P	H	E
U	I	E	A	O	E	E	I	M	R
S	S	R	K	K	R	L	N	S	N

WORKOUT 167
PATHFINDER

T	Y	A	H	S	E	D	O	T	R	E
R	D	T	S	A	L	D	E	E	P	D
E	N	I	L	I	N	K	R	C	M	N
K	U	O	T	L	H	S	L	E	E	A
B	O	E	P	S	U	F	F	Y	R	A
R	E	P	M	S	E	C	N	E	B	M
A	M	L		T	E	F	U	S	L	E
U	B	P	O	R	K	L	O	O	M	S
L	O	M	L	H	I	W	H	C	R	T
A	T	S	I	K	L	A	E	M	A	R
T	E	S	C	U	T	T	L	E	D	I

MOSEY, RAMBLE, STRIDE,
MARCH, WALK, HIKE,
FLOUNCE, STROLL, STOMP,
LIMP, SLINK, SHUFFLE, CREEP,
MEANDER, TODDLE, SASHAY,
TREK, BOUND, TIPTOE,
PERAMBULATE, SCUTTLE

SPOT THE SUM

1 23 (7+16) 2 27 (4+23)

OPPOSITES ATTRACT

1 Follow/lead 2 Double/half
3 Active/passive 4 Extend/
retract 5 Obedient/rebellious

WORKOUT 168
DOMINOES

1 Pamela 2 Graeme 3 Goldie
4 Arnold 5 Stuart 6 Petula

SUDOKU

6	8	7	1	4	9	2	3	5
3	9	5	8	6	2	4	1	7
1	4	2	3	5	7	8	6	9
9	1	8	6	2	4	5	7	3
7	3	6	5	8	1	9	2	4
2	5	4	7	9	3	1	8	6
5	6	9	2	7	8	3	4	1
8	7	3	4	1	5	6	9	2
4	2	1	9	3	6	7	5	8

CODEWORDS

1 Dock 2 Crew 3 Keel 4 Hold
5 Rudder (9=W, 10=L, 11=H,
12=U)

WORKOUT 169
NUMBER JIG

1 298 2 635 3 6402 4 5034

WORDSEARCH

LETTER SEQUENCE

1 J (alternate +5, -3) 2 D (-2,
-3, -4...) 3 S (+2, -4, +6, -8...)
4 S (initial letters of numbers
– well done if you got this)
5 M (+2, +1, +3, +2...)

WORKOUT 170
WILD WORDS

1 Age before beauty 2 North
Star 3 On the up 4 Full house

SMART SUMS

1 56 (60-4) 2 20 (14+6) 3 24
(3x8) 4 5 (10÷2) 5 36 (6x6)

KAKURO

	5	9	7	8			9	7
5	7	8	9	6	3	1	4	2
8	9			9	6	3	8	

WORKOUT 171
ARROWORD

U		A	R			D
S	I	D	E	I	S	S	U	E
E		S		P	A	P		T
A	D	D		P	R	O	S	E
C	A	P		L	A	N	E	S
A	R	O	S	E		G	E	T
R	E	P		S	L	E	D	S

SMALL CHANGE
1 Drill, Hammer, Wrench, Saw, Plane **2** Ravel, Bach, Bizet, Handel, Brahms **3** Shatter, Smash, Break, Snap, Crack **4** Stage, Curtain, Play, Cast, Gods

FUTOSHIKI

2	1	3
1	3	2
3	2	1

WORKOUT 172
FIX SIX

MOBILE CODE
1 Tie **2** String **3** Ribbon **4** Cotton **5** Stomach

FOUR BY FOUR

C	O	R	K
A	M	E	N
P	I	L	E
S	T	Y	E

WORKOUT 173
SPOT THE SUM
1 18 (5+13) **2** 29 (13+16)

SPLITS
1 Bobsleigh **2** Newsagent **3** Grievance **4** Doughnuts **5** Neutrally

TAKE FIVE

M	U	F	T	I
U		A		N
F	A	T	A	L
T		A		E
I	N	L	E	T

WORKOUT 174
MINI JIGSAW
Medway, Severn, Thames, Liffey, Jordan, Humber

KILLER SUDOKU

3	8	2	9	7	1	6	5	4
9	7	5	3	4	6	1	8	2
6	4	1	8	2	5	7	9	3
5	1	4	6	8	9	2	3	7
2	6	8	4	3	7	9	1	5
7	9	3	1	5	2	8	4	6
8	3	9	2	6	4	5	7	1
1	5	6	7	9	3	4	2	8
4	2	7	5	1	8	3	6	9

WORKOUT 175
LOGICAL
Barry, Dracula, 3rd
Harry, Tarzan, 1st
Larry, Superman, 2nd

STAIRCASE
Film set, costume, biopic, X-rated, bit part, montage, outtake.

The "staircase" reveals: FOOTAGE

WORD BUILDER
Amber, Brace, Break, Bench, Baker, Rehab, Backer, Banker, Branch, Embark, Camber, Breach, Chamber, Bracken, Benchmark

WORKOUT 176
OPPOSITES ATTRACT
1 LIGHT and DARK
2 BEFORE and AFTER
3 PROUD and ASHAMED
4 COARSE and REFINED

SET SQUARE

7	+	8	−	6
+		+		x
9	−	2	+	1
÷		÷		÷
4	+	5	÷	3

IN AND OUT
Tramp (+ M), scut (- O), roué (+ U), mere (- T), bathed (+ H)
MOUTH

Put (- O), gape (- R), tier (- G), wheat (+ A), brine (+ N)
ORGAN

WORKOUT 177
WORDSEARCH

THREE IN ONE
1 Port **2** Bolt **3** Watch **4** Banger **5** Match

CELL BLOCKS

SOLUTIONS

WORKOUT 178
SUDOKU

4	1	3	2
3	2	1	4
2	3	4	1
1	4	2	3

2	4	3	1
3	1	2	4
1	3	4	2
4	2	1	3

4	1	2	3
2	3	4	1
1	2	3	4
3	4	1	2

ADD UP
1 30

2 47

3 52

WORKOUT 179
CODEWORD

SO COMPLETE

Idle	Lend	Bard	D
Torn	Polo	Over	O
Laze	Zeal	Jazz	Z
Bear	Chew	Here	E
Town	Scan	Acne	N

WORKOUT 180
NUMBER JIG

Leftover number: **2518**

WORKOUT 181
SCRAMBLE
1 Owl 2 Goose 3 Penguin
4 Falcon 5 Starling
6 Pheasant 7 Albatross
8 Woodpecker

INITIALS
1. Statue of Liberty
2. Lily-of-the-Valley
3. *The Merchant of Venice*
4. *Paint It Black*
5. King Charles Spaniel

HONEYCOMB
1 Before 2 Coffee 3 Scrawl
4 Bellow 5 Search
6 Camera 7 Narrow
8 Catnap 9 Negate
10&11 Free of charge

WORKOUT 182
FITWORD

Narrator

MINI JIGSAW
Bronte, Greene, Huxley
Alcott, Orwell, Conrad

WORKOUT 183
PATHFINDER

RAMSAY MACDONALD, EDEN, CHAMBERLAIN, WALPOLE, PEEL, ATTLEE, DOUGLAS-HOME, MACMILLAN, WILSON, MAJOR, LLOYD GEORGE, EARL GREY, BALDWIN, PALMERSTON, ASQUITH

NUMBER JIG
1 737 **2** 157 **3** 3949

PAIRS
Boiled egg, boyfriend, courtesy light, custard apple, grand piano, hard cheese, master switch, night school, opera glasses, power station, Sunday best, title fight

MOSS and PLATES yield EPSOM SALTS

WORKOUT 184
MANOR BORN
Photo 1

SUDOKU

7	4	6	2	3	1	5	9	8
2	9	5	4	7	8	1	6	3
1	8	3	9	6	5	7	2	4
8	2	9	5	1	3	6	4	7
6	3	7	8	4	2	9	1	5
4	5	1	7	9	6	3	8	2
9	1	8	3	5	4	2	7	6
5	7	2	6	8	9	4	3	1
3	6	4	1	2	7	8	5	9

SPLITS
1 Automatic 2 Secretary
3 Nocturnal 4 Vegetable
5 Quarterly

WORKOUT 185

WORD BUILDER

Litre, Alert, Tiler, Delta, Later, Ideal, Retail, Mailed, Mallet, Redial, Detail, Miller, Literal, Trailed, Tallied, Trialled, Treadmill

WORD SEARCH

CODEWORDS

1 Sea **2** Crab **3** Coast (9=T)
4 Resort **5** Bathers

WORKOUT 186

SMALL CHANGE

1 Dirk, Dagger, Spear, Mace, Club **2** Big, Large, Grand, Vast, Huge
3 Mango, Next, Oasis, Burton, Gap **4** Spire, Nave, Altar, Crypt, Pew

KAKURO

3	1			2	3	1	5
8	6	7	9	4	1	2	3	5
	2	4	7	1			1	2

WORKOUT 187

ARROWORD

SCRAMBLE

1 Bar **2** Inn **3** Café
4 Bistro **5** Eatery
6 Taverna **7** Hostelry
8 Brasserie

INITIALS

1. *One Foot in the Grave*
2. Wolfgang Amadeus Mozart
3. Hide-and-Seek
4. *You Only Live Twice*
5. A stitch in time saves nine

WORKOUT 188

MINI FIT

1 Tor **2** Den **3** Weak
4 Swat

VOWEL PLAY

1 Violin 2 Trumpet
3 Guitar 4 Accordion
5 Piano 6 Oboe
7 Bassoon 8 Flute
9 Organ 10 Cello

SET SQUARE

4	+	7	−	8
+		−		−
9	+	1	÷	5
−		×		×
2	+	3	+	6

WORKOUT 189

SPOT THE SUM

1 24 (8+16) **2** 26 (4+22)
3 22 (9+13) **4** 33 (12+21)

BOX WISE

1 Con **2** Sha **3** Man **4** Tra
5 Sup **6** Per **7** Cer **8** Ise
9 Mit **10** Res **11** Eal **12** Ult

STAIRCASE

Taggart, Hi-De-Hi!, Spender, Mr Bean, Frasier, Angels, Pop Idol.

The "staircase" reveals: **THE BILL**.

WORKOUT 190

MINI JIGSAW

Mirror, Clutch, Engine Hubcap, Bonnet, Towbar

SIX PACK

More Brain-Training Books available from HarperCollins:

The Times 2 Crossword Book 12

978-0-00-726447-6

The Times Su Doku Book 8

978-0-00-727257-0